Pollock Manufacturing Company Limited

ELECTROHOME
ENVIRONMENTAL SYSTEMS

DICTATOR

Electrohome
PRODUCTS

  Electrohome

CKCO-TV

Display Technologies, Inc.

DEILCRAFT

DOMINION ELECTROHOME INDUSTRIES LIMITED
KITCHENER · ONTARIO

Grimes Radio Corporation
Kitchener, Canada   Limited

L/C

VIKING

"Phonola"

ELECTROHOME

HAWKSVILLE LUMBER

CRCA STEREO FM

CKCO-TV 13

ELECTROHOME Display System

The Phonola Company
of Canada, Limited, Elmira

ELECTROHOME
MOTOR OPERATIONS   DIVISION OF ELECTROHOME LIMITED

PLANAR

DOMINION ELECTROHOME INDUSTRIES LIMITED
KITCHENER   ·   ONTARIO

Deilcraft

126 CFRN
Good Sports

ELECTROHOME
Projection Systems

ELECTROHOME

Visionary Thinking™

AABEX

Sunwapta
BROADCASTING CO. LTD.

CJKE-FM

SERVICE ELECTROHOME

CKCO
TELEVISION

Serenader

Deilcraft

ELECTROHOME
APPLIANCES   DIVISION OF ELECTROHOME LIMITED

ARCADIA

PULWEL

ELECTROHOME
PROJECTION PRODUCTS

DEILCRAFT
ELECTROHOME

MOHAWK

ELECTROHOME DISPLAYSYSTEMS

FLEXSTEEL
FINE UPHOLSTERED FURNITURE

CFRN
TELEVISION

Pollock-Welker Limited
Kitchener, Canada

CKCO-TV
E

DOMINION ELECTROHOME
INDUSTRIES LIMITED
KITCHENER   ONTARIO

ckXM 100
FM STEREO

Electrohome

CAMPBELL

ALBON REPRODUCTIONS

AN Electrohome PRODUCT

PLANAR
PLANAR CIRCUITS

ELECTROHOME
ELECTRONICS

HUMIDAIRE

BBS
CKCO-TV

Electrohome

marantz
ELECTROHOME

CKKW  1090

ODEON
Imported Record Quality

 OKeh
The Record of Quality

TELIDON

Deilcraft

Visionary Thinking:
The Story of Canada's Electrohome

By Raymond Stanton

Canadian Cataloguing in Publication Data

Stanton, Raymond, 1933–
Visionary Thinking: The Story of Canada's Electrohome

Includes bibliographical references and index.
ISBN 0-9681575-0-5

1. Electrohome Limited—History. I. Title.

HD9696.A3C344 1997   338.7'621381   C97-900628-7

Electrohome Limited (Head Office)
809 Wellington Street North
Kitchener, Ontario
Canada N2G 4J6
Tel: (519) 744-7111   Fax: (519) 749-3181
Http://www.electro.com

First Published in 1997 by
Canadian Corporate Histories
262 Manitou Drive, Suite 13
Kitchener, Ontario
Canada N2C 1L3
Tel: (519) 893-3505   Fax: (519) 893-4133

Design and production:
Sue Breen and Chris McCorkindale
McCorkindale Advertising & Design

Research:
Nicola McLaughlin, Sue Breen, Chris McCorkindale

Printing:
Cober Printing Limited, Kitchener

Printed in Canada

Artifact photography by Pirak Studios Limited, Waterloo.
Page 5: Phonola model 783-P
Page 9: 1907 one cent coin
Page 12: Music box
Page 15: Hornless phonograph
Page 19: Tabletop Phonola
Page 23: Otto Heineman trunk
Page 25: Organola
Page 28: Duke phonograph
Page 30: Radio/radio-phonograph grouping
Page 32: Chippendale-style phonograph
Page 37: Grimes Inverse Duplex radio
Page 40: Wells-Gardner radio
Page 52: Humidifier
Page 62: Radio-phonograph
Page 68: Black & white television
Page 74: Mardi-Gras radio-TV-phonograph
Page 77: Picture radios
Page 78: Chinoiserie cabinet TV
Page 137: Atari® Asteroids video game

For corporate history details and information, contact:
Raymond Stanton
Canadian Corporate Histories
262 Manitou Drive, Suite 13
Kitchener, Ontario, Canada N2C 1L3
Tel: (519) 893-3503   Fax: (519) 893-4133

Contents

*Phonola 1936
Model 783-P
25-60 cycle.*

Arthur Bell Pollock
1877-1951

Carl Arthur Pollock
1903-1978

John Albon Pollock
1936-

Introduction

The history of Electrohome is a story which mirrors the development of Canada in the 20th century.

As we observe the 90th anniversary of the founding of our company, we can look back and marvel at the courage and determination of the two men who made it all possible.

The small Ontario community of Berlin was a far different place in 1907 than the Kitchener of today. And yet there are similarities.

Despite almost a century of "progress," there is still a belief in many of the old-fashioned values. Men and women with a gleam in their eyes are passionately committed to the belief that dedication and hard work will turn their good ideas into a thriving business.

Many of them are taking a gamble in the hope of making their dreams comes true, as did my grandfather, Arthur Bell Pollock, and his mechanical genius partner, Alex Welker. They made their dream come true and in the process built the foundation for the thriving contemporary company that is now Electrohome.

This book chronicles the often tumultuous path that led to success. The uncertainties and disappointments experienced by Arthur Bell Pollock and his son, Carl Arthur Pollock—my father—were enough to deter all but the most determined would-be entrepreneur.

Their triumphs and satisfactions are recorded. They show how a home-grown Canadian business can survive an often painful rollercoaster ride and that the right amount of determination and courage can earn a rightful place on the world scene.

This book also serves as a valuable reminder that a business consists of people. My father believed that people were Electrohome's most important asset. "I feel that everyone here works with me. No one works for me." He recognized that ideas were initiated by people and that products were the reflection of the creative and skillful members of the organization.

In the ninety years of its existence, Electrohome has been well-served by the people my father used to call "members." They each have a story to tell and many of their reminiscences are included as colorful "flesh" on the dry bones of fact. Regretfully, in telling these stories, it became obvious that many had to be left untold.

As a way of paying tribute to as many of our people as possible, we have included the names of the members of the Quarter Century Club and listed as many families as we could find who had multiple members—and in most cases—multiple generations who worked at Electrohome.

It is my sincere hope that the many thousands whose lives were at some time intertwined with Electrohome will appreciate this gesture of appreciation for their contribution.

From a struggling two-man business, Electrohome has grown to become a large public corporation with customers around the world. To all our stakeholders, I extend an invitation to share our vision of the future.

John A. Pollock,
Chairman and Chief Executive Officer

CHAPTER ONE

1907-1910 By The Toss Of A Coin

The town hall and market building in the centre of Berlin. It was a thriving manufacturing and commercial centre in 1907 when A.B. Pollock started making hornless phonographs.

The coin glinted as it turned in the sunlight, falling into the outstretched palm of the young man.

"Heads!" He smiled quizzically at the young woman sitting on the garden seat. "We stay and make phonographs."

The year was 1907 and the place was Berlin (later named Kitchener), a bustling industrial community seventy miles southwest of Toronto in Canada's heartland.

Arthur Bell Pollock, later to become known as A.B., could not have known that his fateful coin toss would result in the building of a company that would eventually become a household name across Canada and later span the world as a manufacturer of advanced electronic products and television broadcasting services.

Had the coin turned up tails, A.B. Pollock might have tried his luck selling real estate in the developing Canadian West.

Pollock's wife, Racie, was no doubt relieved at her husband's decision, despite his cavalier gesture. The risks involved in launching a new business in Berlin, surrounded by supportive family and friends, would have seemed minor compared to braving the uncertainties of western Canada.

A.B. Pollock was no stranger to uncertainty. He had left Berlin in 1896, at the age of 19, to seek a better life in the hurly-burly of New York City. There he joined two friends from Berlin High School who were studying music at the Metropolitan Opera. One was Racie's brother,

Charles Harry Boehmer, who went on to international fame as an operatic tenor, using the stage name of Carlo Boehmer. The other was Edward Johnston, who also became an operatic star and later, the general manager of the Metropolitan Opera Company. (The popular Guelph Spring Music Festival in Southern Ontario was started by the Foundation which bears his name).

During his sojourn in New York City, A.B. slept on a park bench, swept floors, worked in a restaurant and delivered pamphlets before finding a clerical job with the YMCA. This was followed by a job as paymaster of a twine company. How he obtained his next, and probably most significant, post is not clear.

His association with the two Metropolitan Opera singers probably brought him into contact with influential business people, one of whom was Tennant Putnam, treasurer of the New York Yacht Club and president of the Manhattan Club. Young Pollock became Putnam's private secretary, which included duties as yacht club secretary. As such, he met some of the richest and most influential businessmen in the world.

One of the men he met was Herman Schroeder, who was trying to market a new-style phonograph with the speaker horn concealed in a wooden cabinet.

In the early 1900s, home entertainment was being transformed. Parlor sing-songs and mechanically-operated music were being replaced by the magic of recorded sound played on the "phonograph." Thomas Edison's original 1878 invention had been improved upon by several other entrepreneurs, including Alexander Graham Bell and Emile Berliner, a German-born American who had developed an improved transmitter or microphone for Bell's telephone.

Berliner's experiments with "talking machines" led him to build a "gramophone" which played recordings made on circular rubber discs instead of Edison's wax-covered cylinders. With Eldridge Johnson, Berliner organized the Victor Talking Machine Company, forerunner of RCA Victor.

In the face of intense competition and sharp legal

maneuvering over patents and the rights to sell recordings, Berliner moved to Canada in 1899. He set up a factory in Montreal and started manufacturing the Gram-o-Phone. Two models were offered, priced at $7.50 and $15, complete with sixteen-inch horn and three records.

An advertisement in the *Canadian Magazine* of December 1900 proclaimed:

"The Gram-o-phone reproduces Sousa's and Godfrey's Band, as well as other leading bands of the world. (Sousa's Band does not play for any other talking machine).

"The Gram-o-phone will reproduce a full Orchestra, Chorus or Church Choir...every instrument...a funny story, an auction sale or the Lord's Prayer."

Although the public welcomed the disc record, major artists were at first reluctant to participate in the new entertainment medium. But an up-and-coming Italian tenor, Enrico Caruso, agreed to make some disc recordings in 1902 and this opened the floodgates. Soon, every major artist of the era was represented on disc and there was great competition among record companies to sign up famous stars to their record label.

Herman Schroeder was having difficulty marketing his invention because of strong competition and a lack of funds.

When A.B. told Schroeder that there were no hornless phonographs being sold in Canada, Schroeder suggested that Pollock should fill the gap. A.B. saw the opportunity to develop a business of his own and in 1906, returned to Berlin, taking with him a supply of Schroeder's spring-wound motors, tone arms and reproducers.

For the young Pollock, it was a heaven-sent oppor-tunity to capitalize on his long-standing interest in music and entertainment and on the business acumen he had developed during his exposure to some of the most entrepreneurial minds in New York.

Even in his childhood, A.B. Pollock had shown a determination to excel. One of ten children born in Linwood, Ontario, a rural village about 25 miles north of Berlin, his diligence with his school work prompted his father to send him to high school in Berlin.

His father, David Pollock, managed a flax mill in Linwood as well as running the general store in the village. He would pay the flax mill workers on Saturdays at the store, which made it very convenient for the workers to do their weekly shopping there. Young A.B. loved to

A.B. kept this photo of Sir Thomas Lipton's yacht racing in Long Island Sound as a souvenir of his days as secretary of the New York Yacht Club.

make change at the till and entertain customers with the wind-up music box sent from the United States by a relative. The music box played 10 selections and must have instilled in A.B. a love of music that was to have a profound effect on his personal life and business career. At the Berlin High School, A.B. made a friend of Harry Boehmer, who was a member of a prominent Berlin manufacturing family. He played soccer with Billie King, later to become the Rt. Hon. W.L. Mackenzie King, who was to achieve fame as Canada's longest-serving prime minister. And he was attracted to Harry's sister, Rachel (always called Racie), who was already making a name for herself as a singer.

This 1880s Swiss-made music box, which belonged to A.B. Pollock's father, was played by A.B. as a child. It is still in the family's possession.

Music was a prominent feature of daily life in the Boehmer household. In addition to Harry and Racie, Papa (Charles S.) Boehmer was always singing. And, to A.B.'s delight, there was a new phonograph with a tin horn which he was allowed to wind up and play recordings.

After graduating from Berlin High School, A.B. had found a job as a book-keeper and clerk in a Berlin dry goods store. But the Berlin of 1896 held few opportunities for him and like many young men of his generation, he had decided to head for New York.

After six years in the bustling metropolis and secure in his Yacht Club job, A.B. returned to Berlin, this time to marry his high school sweetheart, Racie Boehmer. The local newspaper, the *Berlin Record* of September 4, 1902, described the event as "one of the prettiest and most fashionable of this season's weddings" and concluded with the hope "that their wedded life be as free from worries and cares as the bride's singing has been free from flaws."

A year later in 1903, Racie returned to Berlin so that their first, and as it turned out, only child, Carl, could be born in Canada. It was soon after this that A.B. met Herman Schroeder and in 1906, decided to take his young family back to Berlin and launch his new business.

The cautious burghers of Berlin did not share Pollock's excitement about the commercial possibilities of a hornless phonograph. He could not find anyone to invest in his new business, even though "Busy Berlin" was undergoing a period of rapid expansion.

Factories were springing up all over town, most of them conceived and operated by local men. There were breweries and bakeries, button makers, tanneries, shoe manufacturers and furniture makers and many more as a tide of new enterprise swept the town.

In October 1905, Ontario Premier J.P. Whitney opened a Made in Berlin Exhibition and proclaimed: "Today Berlin stands at the head of the procession in the Dominion. Such an occasion has never been known in Canada. I will tell people to come here for lessons in enterprise and progress."

The idea of generating electrical power at Niagara Falls and distributing it over power lines throughout Ontario was being promoted around the province by E.W.B. Snider of St. Jacobs, D.B. Dettweiler of Berlin and Adam Beck of London, who became Sir Adam and served as chairman of Ontario Hydro for many years. Their dream was realized in 1910 when hydro-electric power from the newly-created Ontario Hydro Commission was switched on. The ceremony was held in Berlin to recognize the efforts of these visionaries.

But A.B. Pollock's vision was in danger of evaporating. He didn't have the mechanical skills to assemble the hornless phonograph he saw as the key to his future. He was a salesman and a clerk—not an engineer. He sought out Alex Welker, a young engineer who had helped Milton and Nelson Good build the LeRoy automobile, Canada's first production car, at a small plant at the corner of King and Water Streets in Berlin. Later, he worked for the Berlin Electric Company, which made

dry cell batteries, and the Walter Rumpel Company making water meters. When A.B. Pollock sought him out, he was designing tools and machinery to make other people's products.

He was also a keen cello player and his interest in music no doubt was a factor in his decision to join A.B. in making the hornless phonograph. His engineer's eye saw no obstacle to assembling Schroeder's components and fitting them into a wooden cabinet. Their first machine was a tall oak cabinet with a heavy lid over the turntable mechanism and doors at the front which opened to let out the sound.

The Boehmer family gathered their friends in the parlor of their home to witness the unveiling of this new machine. They were enthusiastic in their praise of its soft sweet tone and its furniture-like design and gave A.B. several orders on the spot.

As word spread about the Pollock hornless talking machine, it reached hostile ears.

The young entrepreneur was faced with a lawsuit alleging infringement of a patent for the Victor Hornless machine. Fortunately for A.B., the lawsuit went in his favor, apparently because Victor had not produced a hornless machine in Canada within 12 months of establishing their patent.

Although he was confident that the public would accept his talking machine, A.B. still had to buy the materials he needed. To generate some cash, he went to

Alex Welker, the engineer who helped A.B. Pollock build the first hornless phonograph, became a partner and was a major contributor to the company's early success.

Motorcade passing the Walper Hotel on King Street as part of 1910 celebrations marking the switching-on of hydro-electric power from Niagara Falls.

Pollock and Welker's hornless phonographs eventually bore the Phonola name.

work selling insurance for H.L. Staebler and Co., a well-known local firm. Racie gave singing lessons and led the choir at the Methodist Church.

A souvenir edition of the *Berlin News Record* of 1908 describes the H.L. Staebler & Co. as one of the oldest insurance agencies in Berlin, established in 1875 by the late J.M. Staebler. "The present firm, comprised of his son, Mr. H.L. Staebler and Mr. Arthur B. Pollock, who joined the business in 1906. They represent a number of the strongest companies in the world in all classes of insurance. They are also sole agents for the celebrated Monarch Typewriter and handle all kinds of typewriter supplies."

It was probably no coincidence that A.B. found himself working with Staebler, who was described in the same newspaper as "a pianist of considerable ability and well-known in musical circles." Once again, A.B.'s interest in music had led him to a timely and significant connection, because his insurance income provided the cash to pay Alex Welker a weekly wage of nine dollars.

As a young single man, Welker had no ties and his enthusiasm kept him working long hours—often well into the night. A.B. would join him after a day of selling insurance and persuading friends and relatives to buy

their phonographs. The reaction of people they approached persuaded them to add a tabletop model to their original full-sized version.

Cabinets were made by a local furniture company and Alex Welker made the tone arms, reproducers and windup motors in rented space in a nearby foundry. The phonographs were assembled in the carriage house of Racie's family home on Queen Street North. A.B. stencilled the trade names on the cabinets, helped pack them for shipping and handled the paperwork.

As word spread about the new machine, A.B. would organize phonograph concerts in nearby towns and villages. The orders began to come in. A.B. expanded his sales territory, tirelessly seeking out retailers willing to give a new Canadian-made product a chance over the better-known American names.

In her 1957 history marking the 50th anniversary of the company, author Edna Staebler recounts this story of his first big order:

A.B. went on a business trip on the train to Winnipeg. He was not a high pressure salesman: he loved to swap stories; people liked him. The manager of the R.S. Williams store said he wanted to give him an order but couldn't without first getting permission from the parent store in Toronto. On A.B.'s instructions, Alex shipped a machine to Toronto. When he visited the Williams store a day or so later he found it unpacked and standing in the store showroom along with some pianos, tin-horn talking machines and other cabinet models imported from the States. (R.S. Williams was the principal Canadian distributor for Edison).

Alex found his way to the office of H.G. Stanton, the company's general manager, a gruff scowling man who glared at the young mechanic in his Sunday blue serge. Alex told him he'd sent a phonograph down from Berlin and he'd like him to have a look at it.

"I'm not interested." The man turned away. "I don't think anyone in Berlin can make a phonograph."

An indignant Alex was emphatic in describing the superior features of his machine. He persuaded Stanton to examine it. Downstairs in the showroom, he asked the sales clerk, "What do you think of it?"

"Why Mr. Stanton sir, I've just sold that machine," the eager clerk replied. "A lady came in here a few minutes ago and seemed to think it was wonderful."

Alex went back to Berlin that night with an order for 25 phonographs. The Pollock Manufacturing Company was really in business.

Full of confidence, the two men rented space from the Hoffman Button Company at 84 Queen Street South, a few blocks from the carriage house. They bought a bench lathe, a drill press and an emery stand. To take supplies to the upper floor and take out finished phonographs, Alex installed a track on which ran a small trolley operated by a winch. Little Carl Pollock took delight in being given a ride up and down the stairs in the trolley.

Three men were hired to assemble the phonographs. Alex continued to work for nine dollars a week—less than the men he'd hired.

Early in 1909, A.B. gave up selling insurance and devoted his considerable energies to increasing sales. He travelled across Canada, convincing retailers to become dealers and taking their orders for his talking machine. He was shrewd enough to see that if people bought a phonograph, they would also want to buy records. He went to Philadelphia and negotiated a deal to import recordings of world-famous entertainers and orchestras.

Orders began to pour in as the Pollock name was advertised and people began to recognize it as a product to be measured against the Victrola and the Edison

versions of the phonograph. Soon, the staff found themselves scrambling to fill the orders.

The growing enterprise took over the whole of the top floor and part of the basement of the button factory. Racie helped out by cataloguing and packing records for shipping. When she found any warped ones, she'd take them home and warm them in the oven to straighten them out.

The Pollock Manufacturing Company Ltd. was formally incorporated on April 21, 1909, with a share capital of $40,000. The documents show that the provisional directors were A.B. Pollock, Charles Stoltz Boehmer, August Boehmer, Alexander Welker and James Pollock of New York, A.B.'s brother. The two Boehmers were Racie's father and his brother, owners of a local box manufacturing company.

The company's oldest advertisement from 1909 lists four models of the Pollock Cabinet Talking Machines: King, Crown Prince, Princess and Duke—"the world's best music by the world's best artists reproduced in the richest, most mellow tone, true as life itself." The advertisement also promotes Star Records—"every record is a gem of perfect recording."

One year later, in 1910, the company moved to a building on Victoria Street North to accommodate their growing business. The two men used a horse-drawn sled to move equipment and material from their overcrowded Queen Street premises.

Berlin was again in the midst of a boom. Eight new factories were started and additions were built to 14 existing ones. "Made in Berlin" was a proudly-affixed label and A.B. was determined that his phonographs would be just as well-known as the furniture, baggage, buttons, boxes, beer and sausages that were pouring out of Berlin and into homes all across Canada.

The red brick building measured 65 by 100 feet and seemed enormous to Alex and A.B. It was at the end of a muddy path on the outskirts of town. One electric motor powered shafts and pulleys for the whole operation, which included a machine shop, a buffing room and a plating room. There was ample space to assemble the phonographs and pack them for shipping, along with the growing stream of record orders they were receiving.

A.B. hired several salesmen and took on more men to make components and assemble phonographs.

Early chronicles depict a happy, carefree workplace.

Pollock Cabinet Talking Machines

MODELS: "King", "Crown Prince", "Princess", "Duke"

The Ideal Home Entertainers

The World's best music by the World's best artists reproduced in the richest, most mellow tone, true as life itself.

All moving parts and the horn are concealed in handsome cabinets of Walnut, Mahogany or Oak.

Star Records

Listen to the "Star" and you will realize its tone is clear, loud and musical. Every Record is a gem of perfect recording. Every selection popular.

MODEL "CROWN PRINCE"

Pollock Manufacturing Company, Berlin, Canada

The company's first advertisement from 1909. Even at this early stage, the company was selling records to be played on its "talking machines."

"When records came in, the men tested them on the new phonographs they had made and danced with the girl in the shipping room. People who worked at Pollock's didn't leave to take other jobs. They were interested in what went on and delighted when there was a big order. They all knew one another and called themselves Pollock's family. At stag picnics with bologna, liverwurst and beer, A.B. took along boxing gloves to amuse the employees. At social gatherings with dancing, Racie led them in singsongs."

As 1910 came to a close, A.B. Pollock, at the age of 33, stood on the threshold of a future filled with promise and hope. His ambition and entrepreneurial drive had pointed the way to success. His perseverance and hard work had overcome the obstacles faced by most fledgling enterprises. He knew now that the coin he had tossed had fallen the right way.

CHAPTER TWO

1911-1917 Phonographs and Furniture

Carl Pollock with his mother, Rachel (Racie) Boehmer Pollock, and father, Arthur Bell Pollock, circa 1916. (opposite)

By then, the tabletop Phonola (above) was popular.

The cheers grew louder as the town hall clock struck the first notes of midnight. The band played a fanfare and as the notes reached a flourishing finale, Mayor W.H. Schmalz clambered on to a chair, an official-looking document in his hands. Gradually the noise subsided as the huge crowd, spilling over the sidewalks and lawns of Berlin's main square, fell silent.

The words so proudly read by the mayor proclaimed the elevation of Berlin from a town to a city. The date was June 10, 1912. The population of "Busy Berlin" had reached 15,000, the number required by the Ontario government in order to bestow cityhood on a municipality.

The Pollock Manufacturing Company was one of the 76 companies in Berlin which between them employed almost 4,000 people. Most of the factories were located within a mile of the centre of town so that people could walk to work.

The men who owned these companies lived in large homes, many of them built in the Italianate style. In their book, *Kitchener: An Illustrated History*, historians John English and Ken McLaughlin wrote of these men:

"These businessmen were conspicuous examples of what initiative, perseverance and energy could accomplish and they kept alive a sense of community in Berlin, long after the economic and social results of industrialization had created deep divisions in many other urban communities. For as Berliners themselves

proudly boasted, there were no sections of town where grand homes might not be found."

Civic boosters swelled with pride as they read the chorus of congratulation expressed in newspapers across Canada in such lavishly-worded editorials as these:

"There is much to admire in the citizens of Berlin, especially their public spirit, their indomitable industry and enterprise and their business acumen. If every other city developed the same spirit of co-operation and local loyalty as Berlin, every such city would progress much faster."

"Berlin is certainly one of the most prosperous and thrifty municipalities in Canada."

"The secret of Berlin's success is that everybody works."

Despite such "progress", most of Berlin's streets remained unpaved. Horses were used for delivery work—only the most progressive businesses were experimenting with motor trucks—and there were only 180 automobiles in use. That was enough, however, for the town council to furnish police officers with stop watches to record the speed of fast drivers.

When Elma Detwiler was hired in 1912 as the company's first full-time female employee, she had to walk along muddy streets to get to work. She told of having to wear rubber overshoes until May. One of the workmen had the job of cleaning off the dirty rubbers each day.

She was given a desk in one corner of the main floor where the phonographs were assembled. The salesmen would bring their orders and pick up their pay cheques from Miss Detwiler, who was Mr. Pollock's stenographer, payroll clerk and general office helper.

The automobile, the telephone, hydro-electric power and the phonograph were among the innovations transforming the daily lives of Canadians. In a 1912 diary kept by Gordon Eby, a self-employed market gardener, he described the excitement when the telephone was installed in his home. He also revealed the hard-headed attitude of Berliners even toward products made in their own community as he told of how he looked into the phonographs available to him before he made his choice.

As the popularity of talking machines grew, they arrived in Canada by the carload, mainly from United States manufacturers but also from Britain.

Eby's diary illustrates why The Pollock Manufacturing Company found it tough to compete against these well-advertised big name brands.

He recorded that he "inspected, first, the Pollock cabinet gramophone at Jaimet's and the Edison model at a friend's, Will Mitchell."

The Edison distributors in Winnipeg sent him their catalogue. He decided against buying an Edison or a Triumph with an oak horn which he saw in Dresden's store in Waterloo. Unfortunately, he omitted the name of the "machine" he did buy, (likely a Victrola, made in Montreal by Emile Berliner's company). He obtained it from the Wanless store, along with a selection of records. He also related how he bought some blank records and how he used these to record his own voice.

In the face of such competition, A.B. Pollock looked around for alternative sources of revenue.

The attainment of cityhood and the optimistic predictions of growth gave him the inspiration he needed. The big new factory was not being used to its full capacity. After the cramped conditions of their Queen Street South premises, the 65 by 100 foot space seemed immense, particularly with only a handful of employees.

A city planning committee was forecasting a population of 50,000 and A.B.'s creative mind reasoned that the new homes that would be built for these people would require bathroom fittings of various kinds—fittings that could easily be made when his men were not busy making phonograph parts. He and the resourceful Alex Welker adapted the machinery that made tone arms so that it could turn out nickel-plated brass towel bars, toothbrush and tumbler holders, soap dishes and toilet paper holders. The men who plated and polished phonograph parts could do the same for this new line of products.

It was a sideline that helped bring in revenue to finance the on-going expansion of the phonograph business.

The manufacture of bathroom accessories as well as phonograph components laid the groundwork for the

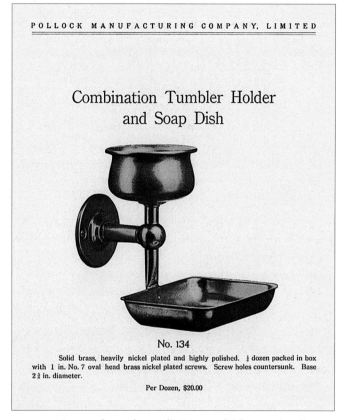

POLLOCK MANUFACTURING COMPANY, LIMITED

Combination Tumbler Holder and Soap Dish

No. 134

Solid brass, heavily nickel plated and highly polished. ¼ dozen packed in box with 1 in. No. 7 oval head brass nickel plated screws. Screw holes countersunk. Base 2⅝ in. diameter.

Per Dozen, $20.00

A catalogue described the company's bathroom fittings as "neat in design, highly polished, strong and durably made. The quality and weight of the brass used, the perfect construction, together with the high quality of the nickel-plating, are points to which particular attention is directed."

company's metal products division, which remained at the Victoria Street North premises for many decades, turning out an assortment of products that would have impressed A.B.

Alex Welker had similar ideas. He used the expertise of his employees in the machine shop to develop a business making tools for other manufacturers in the area.

These were timely moves and ones which set a pattern that was to be followed for many years to come: Identify and exploit an opportunity for growth in a field in which the company had related expertise or capacity.

It was a strategy—an approach—that was used many times to propel the company to higher levels of achievement.

A.B. Pollock also saw opportunities for phonograph sales outside Canada, particularly in countries where the phonograph was not being made. The fact that he had fewer than 20 employees obviously did not deter him and he promoted the company vigorously. Elma Detwiler later recalled an extensive export business with customers in Australia, New Zealand and Mexico.

Even though Alex Welker was engaged in a constant search for improvements to the phonograph business, his energetic nature led him to renew his interest in the design and manufacture of an automobile.

He went into partnership with Herman W. Doerr to produce a two-cylinder powered car which they named the Welker Doerr and sold for $400. Unfortunately, a combination of competition from other makers and the outbreak of the First World War put an end to their dreams of an automobile empire. Their company spent the war years making ammunition and eventually faded from the scene.

In 1913, A.B. decided that the company needed more products to sell. He and Racie, who spoke the language, sailed to Germany to visit the Carl Lindstrom Company in Berlin. The company made gramophones with large and beautifully decorated metal horns but it was their recordings that A.B. had his eye on.

Lindstrom made records in many different languages and had recording contracts with many famous artists. A.B. wanted access to this supply of top quality entertainment, which he felt would enhance the value of his phonographs. He also expressed an interest in buying phonograph components made by Lindstrom, including spring motors, sound boxes, tone arms, horns and mounting brackets, and the needles which picked up the recorded sound.

Subsequently, the Lindstrom organization sent their sales manager, Otto Heineman, on a sales mission to North America. He arrived in Berlin, Ontario, with six heavy trunks containing samples of spring motors and phonograph accessories. It was toward the end of July, 1914.

Heineman's sales mission came to an abrupt end before it got properly started. With the outbreak of war, he suddenly found himself in unfriendly territory. He cancelled his sales trip and with the help of A.B. Pollock, entered the still-neutral United States at Niagara Falls, posing as a sightseer. He left behind his six sample trunks. One of them is still in the company's possession. Heineman remained in the United States and was later to emerge as a significant figure in the home entertainment business, with a special association with A.B. Pollock.

The visit to Germany was not the only evidence of A.B.'s determination to become a major player in the Canadian phonograph business. By this time, the company was making four tabletop phonographs and three large cabinet versions. To complement them, the company, in a 1914 advertisement in a trade publication, announced the addition of three new record labels. A history of the recording industry (*Roll Back the Years, History of Canadian Recorded Sound and Its Legacy*, by Edward B. Moogk) tells the story of the records, imported from Britain and Italy:

This is one of six trunks left behind by Otto Heineman in 1914. It was found in a storage area at Electrohome's Kitchener headquarters during research for this book. Inside were samples of spring motors and other phonograph accessories made by the German company which Heineman represented.

THE PHONOLA **PLUS** OUR RECORD
PROPOSITION   PROPOSITION

Gives the retailer the unbeatable, unapproachable
opportunity in the talking machine world of Canada.

FONOTIPIA   ODEON   JUMBO

THE POLLOCK MFG. CO., Limited
Manufacturers of the PHONOLA
BERLIN - - CANADA
WHOLESALE DISTRIBUTORS
WHALEY, ROYCE & CO., Ltd., Toronto   The NATIONAL TALKING MACHINE CO., Ltd., Winnipeg

*Trade publication
advertisement
announcing the
company's
acquisition of
three new
record labels.*

"The Pollock Mfg. Co. of Berlin (Kitchener), Ontario, announced in June 1914 that it secured exclusive rights in Canada and Newfoundland for Fonotipia, Odeon and Jumbo records. The company was already in the talking machine business with its Phonola line, and thanks to this latter move, it would specialize entirely in recorded sound. Pollock's first record catalogue featured such outstanding artists and ensembles as Alessandro Bonci, John McCormack... the band of H.M. Grenadier Guards..."

The outbreak of the war dramatically changed the complexion of business for A.B. Pollock and his staff. His trip to Germany had obviously been wasted, but more serious than that was the almost immediate decrease in sales of phonographs. The only bright spot, from a business standpoint, was the public's enthusiastic purchase of recordings of patriotic songs.

According to Edward Moogk:

"Canada's entry in World War I set off a nationwide wave of patriotic fervor and nowhere was it more manifest than in music and song. Canadians sang and listened to patriotic songs in the great concert halls and theatres of the big urban centres and in the church basements and lodge meeting places of the smaller communities; they listened to stirring airs by marching bands; they bought sheet music; and they demanded records. Sensing a bonanza, the industry produced a veritable flood of discs recorded at home and abroad.

"The Pollock Company imported from Great Britain the time-honoured songs recorded by British artists including Tommy Atkins, Soldiers of the King, Hearts of Oak, La Marseillaise, La Brabanconne, and The Red, White and Blue.

"Through the Odeon label, Pollock also issued three double-sided recordings by the Band of the 106th Battalion, Light Infantry of Winnipeg, the only one to accompany the First Canadian Contingent to Britain up to that point."

Although the war resulted in a decline in phonograph production, Alex Welker's never-ending search for improvements led him to develop a new type of spring-powered motor for their products. He named it the Helycon and protected it by obtaining patents on its design.

He also completed his experiments with a new idea in sound reproduction to replace the "reproducer" they imported from Connecticut, which tended to sound squeaky when high notes were played. His idea was "based on the principles of the pipe organ and applied in a manner that would amplify and purify the tones produced." Resonating tubes were "employed in varied sizes determined by scientific calculation" to produce a mellow tone. Welker patented the design and incorporated it in a Phonola model called the Organola.

A 1915 advertisement said the Organola "unquestionably takes front rank among the truest, clearest, purest and sweetest tone possible to reproduce." The advertisement listed the Pollock company's wholesale distributors for eastern and western Canada, another indication of its stature in the industry.

Harry Pope, who joined the firm in early 1915, told how it took three men one week to turn out an Organola. The turntables on the better models were covered in purple or green velvet and the tone arms and some other parts were gold plated.

"The gold was taken out of the office safe, weighed before it was used and then weighed again at the end of the day to see how much had been used."

Harry worked with Bill Shelley in inspection, a job he took over shortly afterwards when Shelley was moved to shipping and receiving. Harry was in charge of the inspection department for many years.

In Berlin, young men flocked to enlist in the 118th Battalion, including several from the Pollock firm. They were billeted in a factory and underwent their initial training in Victoria Park. Racie Pollock was one of numerous civilians who did their bit by working for the Red Cross and the Imperial Order of Daughters of the Empire (IODE). Overall, there was great excitement before the grim reality of war cast an air of gloom over the town.

A.B. Pollock was gloomy, too. He saw his successful business evaporating as sales plummeted. But his mood did not last for long. He made use of his extensive network of personal and business contacts to find ways of putting the plant's manufacturing capabilities to wartime use.

The immediate result was a government order for 100,000 exploders for shells. Alex Welker figured out how to make them and A.B. rounded up some second-hand

machinery. They hired nine toolmakers and went into production.

Suddenly, the factory was busy again. The successful completion of the first order was followed by others as the voracious appetite of the conflict in Europe kept armament manufacturers working at full capacity. The company received contracts to make fuses, base plugs and adapters for shells, and motorcycle lamps painted black for military dispatch riders.

By 1916, with the war in Europe taking its awful toll, the once-proud name of Berlin had become a liability. Canadians were refusing to buy goods that were marked Made in Berlin. Many of the city's manufacturers reported anti-German feelings as the reason for orders being cancelled.

Even the community was divided. While many of the young men who had gone off to fight had German-sounding names, their loyalty was not in question. For some hotheads, however, anything with a German connection was fair game for their attacks. A statue of

The Organola, introduced in 1915, featured resonating tubes to produce a mellow tone. It was announced as "the greatest advance in talking machine construction since the beginning of the industry."

Kaiser Wilhelm which had stood in Victoria Park for many years was torn from its base and thrown into the muddy waters of the lake by a rowdy gang as a demonstration of their loyalty to the Allied cause. The statue was fished out of the water and taken for safe-keeping to the Concordia Club, the city's long-established German club. Soon afterwards, it disappeared and has never been found.

The loss of business by local companies prompted a move to change the name of the community. The proposal was hotly-debated and feelings ran high. In the end, the supporters of a name change were able to push through a plebiscite in which voters were offered the choice of six names: Brock, Kitchener, Corona, Adanac, Keowana and Benton.

By a narrow majority, the name of Kitchener was selected. Instead of a name which reflected the community's early beginnings, the city now bore the name of a British hero, Lord Kitchener, who drowned at sea in 1916. While the arguments continued and people got used to the idea of saying they came from Kitchener, they put aside

their feelings and went back to the task of helping to win the war.

By September of that year, the staff had grown from six employees to about 50 to handle the wartime contracts. One newcomer was Bertha Becker, who joined Miss Detwiler as the only female employees. She was hired by A.B. Pollock at a salary of $5 a week, following an interview at which the "shy" Miss Becker was accompanied by her mother.

"We worked five and a half days a week in 1915—sometimes a full six. We started at 8:30 a.m. and worked until 5 p.m. Very often we had to work in the evenings. When this happened, Mr. Pollock would always walk with me to the uptown area and see that I was safely on the street car."

Miss Becker said A.B. Pollock was on the road most of the time in those days. Back in town, he would organize steak parties and picnics for the men. She described her boss as "a grand person—I never heard him say a cross word to anyone.

"If at times he was upset and dictated a letter with

Wartime contracts resulted in a rapid increase in staff. When the war broke out, there were only six employees, including two women, Elma Detwiler (hired in 1912), and Bertha Becker, who started in 1915. This circa 1917 photo shows over 90 people, including several women.

a little sarcasm in it, I wouldn't mail it out because I knew sooner or later he would ask me to destroy it and he would dictate another.

"Just before my first vacation, Mr. Pollock gave me an envelope containing a present and told me not to open it until I got home. When I did open it, I found twenty-five dollars, which was an awful lot of money in those days."

Soon after joining the firm, Miss Becker was put in charge of the payroll, a job she kept for 45 years. The practice then was to pay employees in cash and Mr. Pollock would withdraw the required amount each week from the bank. On one of his trips to the bank, a friend offered him a ride back to the Victoria Street plant. He stuffed the cash, about $2,000, in his pocket and got in the car. The friend dropped him off at a corner near the plant. When he arrived at the office, he reached into his pocket. The cash was not there!

"I couldn't begin to describe the look on his face at that moment," Miss Becker later recalled.

A.B. retraced his steps and found the money, lying in the road where he had got out of his friend's car.

By 1917, with no end in sight to the war, there were two shifts operating at full capacity on contracts. The United States entered the war that year and Pollock Manufacturing started making shell adapters for the U.S. Army. Alex Welker had to make two trips to New York in the course of fulfilling this contract. This resulted in a visit to the factory by an Army official, whose job was to examine the company's accounts to ensure that the military were not being over-charged. When he came

to Welker's expense account for his New York visits, the officer exclaimed: "How the devil can a fellow make a trip to New York for only thirty-eight dollars?"

The production of Phonolas continued on a limited scale. A.B. Pollock knew that when the war ended, there would be a rapid escalation of demand as people resumed normal activities and indulged in their growing passion for recorded music.

He and Alex Welker decided that it was time to manufacture their own wooden cabinets for their phonographs. They started looking for suitable premises and found them in Elmira, a small farming community 10 miles to the north. It might be more appropriate to say that Elmira found them, since the trustees of the village passed special legislation to enable the company to take over the premises and equipment of an idle woodworking plant.

It was ideal—a 2 1/2 acre site on which stood a three-storey brick factory, 125 feet long and 50 feet wide, with both electric and steam power. The steam was essential for the kilns which would be used to dry the oak, walnut and mahogany used for the phonograph cabinets.

Equipment was moved in and Edgar Schaub was hired as foreman of the new furniture and woodworking division. As he hired the first of the 30 employees who were to start up the new operation, an addition was built, 50 feet wide by 100 feet long, to house the trimming, assembling, packing and shipping departments.

Most of the work was done by hand and a good week's production amounted to about 100 cabinets. A

1917 catalogue listed four tabletop models ranging in price from $18 to $65 and six large cabinet models, priced from $75 for the Duchess to $250 for the Organola.

The advertisement describes the "beautiful finish and design" of the wooden cabinets and boasts that the Organola's resonating pipes and concealed winding crank "are really the only new ideas in the Phonograph in years."

The aggressive tone of the advertisement no doubt reflected the fiercely competitive nature of the phonograph business in Canada. The expiry of patents owned by Berliner, Edison and Columbia opened the door to a flock of companies eager for a share of this obviously-lucrative marketplace. Competitors for Pollock's Phonola sprang up in Toronto, Hamilton, Stratford, Owen Sound and London, as well as in several other Canadian cities.

In his book, *Roll Back the Years*, Edward Moogk writes: "Despite the proliferating competition, the Berliner Gramophone Company continued to do a roaring business. At the beginning of 1917, it was unable to take on any new dealers even though production of records and gramophones had increased by 279 percent."

There was also a great deal of activity around the production of records, with different methods of recording resulting in records that were "lateral cut" or "vertical cut" (the latter being played from the inside out).

A "lateral cut" record made in Montreal for the Phonola Company.

Edward Moogk again:

"Meanwhile, in one of the established companies, there was a major development. In March 1918, C.J. Pott, Canadian sales manager for the Otto Heineman Phonograph Supply Company, returned to Toronto following a week-long sales meeting with the parent company in New York.

"Also attending the same gathering was A.B. Pollock of the Pollock Manufacturing Company of Kitchener. Shortly after, Pollock began advertising a line of records that were pressed from Heineman masters. These records were of the hill-and-dale style, played with a sapphire ball, similar to the Pathe (brand).

"Two months later, the Phonola Company of Canada Ltd. was formed to take over Pollock's record business. The Phonola Company continued Pollock's practice of pressing records from Otto Heineman masters, and the first line of records advertised by the Phonola Company was manufactured in this way; it was called the Phonola line. (The actual pressing was carried out for Phonola in Lachine, near Montreal, by Herbert Berliner's Compo Company).

"In the fall of 1919, the General Phonograph Corporation of New York, formerly known as the Otto Heineman Phonograph Supply Company Inc., announced

This 1916 Duke was one of several models with handsome wooden cabinets made at the company's new woodworking plant in Elmira.

Circa 1919 photo shows Victoria Street plant bearing the company's new name, General Phonograph Corporation of Canada.

that it had purchased Pollock's phonograph factory in Kitchener. A.B. Pollock was to remain manager of the factory, while Canadian sales operations were to be continued under the management of C.J. Potts. The Heineman and Meisselbach phonograph motors, as well as their tone arms and sound boxes, were to be imported from the United States and assembled at the factory."

The Heineman behind this transaction was the same man A.B. Pollock had escorted safely over the border into the United States in 1914. Now here he was joining forces with the man who had befriended him at a time when he needed help.

Company records provide no explanation of this move. The most likely explanation is that Pollock and Welker wanted to take advantage of the booming market for phonograph records, specially the bonanza they expected when the war ended.

To compete with the likes of Edison and the Berliner Company, they apparently forged a relationship with Heineman. This would have provided not only the capital but also a connection with an influential U.S. distributor.

It appears that Heineman's purchase of the Victoria Street factory did not affect operations in Elmira, where cabinets were produced and phonographs assembled and shipped.

This arrangement was to last for only six years.

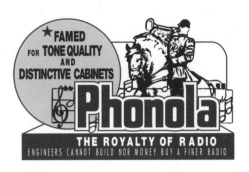

CHAPTER THREE

1918-1932 The Age of Radio

Three console radios and a radio-phonograph combination (left) made in the 1920s. Their elaborately-crafted wooden cabinets were similar to those made for the company's phonographs.

The headphones crackled and A.B. Pollock jumped. A moment later, he heard the faint voice, excitedly describing a boxing bout. He listened for a moment and handed the earphones back to his son, Carl, and smiled indulgently.

"There might be something in it, do you think, Alex?" he said, looking across the table to his partner.

Alex Welker grunted. "I'm not convinced."

It was July 4, 1919, and the Pollock clan had gathered around the crystal radio set made by Carl, then 15. He was proudly demonstrating his new-found knowledge by tuning into the broadcast of the world heavyweight championship fight between Jack Dempsey and Jess Willard.

Little did A.B. know that those far-off sounds were going to transform their phonograph business—and much sooner than they could imagine.

The end of the war on November 11, 1918, had brought about the increasing demand for home entertainment products that A.B. Pollock had anticipated. The two factories had quickly turned away from the war work that had kept them busy and resumed production of an increasing array of phonographs.

An employee of that time wrote:

"More and better machines, acquired during the war, were available. There were batteries of turret lathes, newer and better gear cutting equipment, a number of multi-spindle drill presses, special tapping machines and a better-equipped toolroom.

This elegant Chippendale-style phonograph, made in 1919, was typical of the luxury items people wanted after the austere war years.

"After four years of wartime austerity, the people were quite willing to spend their savings on luxury items such as a new phonograph. Sales of phonograph records boomed and Mr. Pollock was ready to fill the demand."

Components made at the Victoria Street plant were exported around the world—30,000 small, spring-wound motors to China, tone arms and reproducers to Australia, Helycon motors to Mexico and an assortment of parts to England, France and New Zealand.

How the company obtained these orders remains a mystery. It seems logical to assume that they resulted from a combination of A.B.'s business network and connections established during the fulfillment of wartime contracts, even though the federal government was not actively encouraging the export of anything but Canada's natural resources. The company was still controlled by Heineman's General Phonograph Corp. in New York, which may have been the source of these orders.

The firm's export business made A.B. a natural choice as a member of the export committee of the Phonograph Manufacturers Association at its inaugural meeting at the King Edward Hotel in Toronto on September 25, 1919.

Another development which created sales on a national level was the manufacture of phonographs bearing the name of a retail outlet, a practice subsequently known as "private brand" manufacturing. As a result, phonographs assembled in Elmira could be found in Eaton's department stores across Canada, and in numerous other retail outlets who wanted their own name attached to such a popular product.

Operating on a national scale like this prompted the company to open its own retail stores in Toronto and Winnipeg, as well as a store located at the corner of King and William Streets in downtown Waterloo.

As orders increased, more staff had to be hired. The Elmira plant soon had 40 people making Phonolas and shipping phonograph records and needles to a population clamoring for musical entertainment.

One of those hired to handle the expanding list of orders was John Koegler, a recent German immigrant. He was relieved to find that half the people he worked with spoke German.

John Koegler

Koegler was paid 30 cents an hour when he started, even though he had been trained in Germany as a "fine mechanic." By contrast, some mechanics, particularly those who had enjoyed high wages during the war, were paid as much as 75 cents an hour.

Despite his misgivings, he spent the next 48 years with the company and retired in 1972 as chief inspector and technical advisor for the Electric Motor Division.

In later years, he collected and recorded historical information about the company's early years.

He provided this description of working life in 1921. "About 10 men rode bicycles to work and parked them inside the plant near the punch clock.

"One car, a 1920 Hudson, was usually parked on the street right in front of the office door. It belonged to Mr. A.B. Pollock. He used it to travel to Elmira, where our woodworking plant was located. Occasionally, Alex Welker, our superintendent, would bring his Franklin to work and park it in some shady spot.

"We did not have a parking problem! A few regular employees owned a car but they used it for Sunday afternoons only. As soon as the first snow fell, they would remove the wheels and store the car until the following spring.

"To build a phonograph required a spring-type motor, a tone arm, a soundbox or a reproducer, and a cabinet. The first three items plus all necessary hardware were produced at the main plant on Victoria Street.

"We made phonograph motors in various styles and sizes, differing mainly in the numbers of springs used. The largest motor would play three 10-inch records or two 12-inch records, or a total of about eight minutes.

"Our Helycon motors were a much simpler design

A trade magazine advertisement from the company's Toronto agents featured the Helycon phonograph motor, developed by Alex Welker.

(than those imported from the U.S. and other countries), requiring only two gears and two worms for the drive. Two simple spiral gears were used to wind up the springs by means of a crank. Helycon was our registered trade mark and used for our phonograph motors and related accessories.

"Reproducers were continuously improved upon by our own craftsmen. Earlier models were diecast of aluminum or white metal and used mica diaphragms. The phonograph needles had to be changed every two records and were available for soft, medium and loud reproduction. Sound was reproduced and amplified by mechanical means only. The tracks in the records were much deeper and more widely spaced to allow for high mechanical amplitude" (which increased the output of sound).

"The sound box was fastened to the tone arm which carried the sound into the built-in horn. The original tone arms were made by an ingenious but costly method. The shape was cast out of lead, and poured into split molds. The core was then cleaned and polished and hung overnight in a copper plating solution. The plated core was placed in a bath of hot lead, melting the lead core, leaving a copper shell.

"Later, we developed new equipment and methods to make better tone arms faster and cheaper using brass tubing.

Tone arms were among several components sold to other phonograph manufacturers around the world.

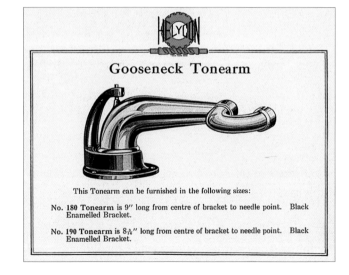

HELYCON

Gooseneck Tonearm

This Tonearm can be furnished in the following sizes:

No. 180 Tonearm is 9" long from centre of bracket to needle point.   Black Enamelled Bracket.

No. 190 Tonearm is 8¾" long from centre of bracket to needle point.   Black Enamelled Bracket.

Phonograph components were delivered to the Kitchener railway station to be shipped to Elmira for assembly.

"Motors, sound boxes, tone arms and related metal products were shipped to the Elmira plant by Grand Trunk Railroad, which made these trips from Kitchener daily, carrying passengers, express and freight on the same train."

Back on a peacetime footing in 1919, the population went back to work and started spending money again. Soldiers who had fought in the war had been exposed to a great variety of music and came home expecting to enjoy the same kind of entertainment. While the demand for home entertainment products such as the Phonola and a wide variety of records continued to be strong, it was affected by soaring prices and inflation. The resulting general economic downturn in the early 1920s made the predictions of some industry leaders appear somewhat optimistic.

The industry explored ways to stimulate sales, taking advantage of every innovation and technical advance.

In Kitchener, A.B. Pollock and Alex Welker studied

developments in the design of the phonograph as an item of furniture. Designers and furniture builders were reaching new heights of artistic excellence in introducing console-type models in place of the popular upright models.

One new idea was the portable phonograph. A.B. and Alex Welker quickly introduced the Pulwel Portable, which was sold in the company's retail stores and made available to other retailers through distributors.

A development which was to have a profound effect on the phonograph business was the introduction of electrical recording using a microphone. This process, which made acoustical horn recording obsolete, was invented in 1919 and developed by Lionel Guest, a British financier who served as aide-de-camp to Lord Minto, Canada's Governor-General, and Horace O. Merriman, a native of Hamilton and a graduate of the University of Toronto.

The first public demonstration of their microphone recording apparatus took place in Westminster Abbey in London, when they recorded the funeral service for the Unknown Warrior on Armistice Day in 1920.

The need to promote the sale of records and phonographs became stronger as the threat from radio broadcasting as an entertainment medium became more apparent. Two-sided recordings were introduced as a means of generating more business. Many record companies, including Phonola, reduced the price of records from $1 to 85 cents and some as low as 65 cents.

The advent of radio was something the phonograph industry could not ignore.

In Montreal, the Canadian Marconi Company's broadcasting station XWA (later CFCF) had begun test broadcasts as early as 1918 and again, on a more regular basis in 1919, making it the first regularly operated broadcasting station in the world. In 1920, the Berliner Gramophone Company broadcast a Victrola concert from the Marconi station, featuring His Majesty's Voice records.

By 1920, a year after the 15-year-old Carl Pollock

had proudly shown off his crystal radio, Americans were listening to regular programs of music and speech from KDKA in Pittsburgh, UBZ in Springfield, Illinois, and WGR in Schenectady, New York.

During the First World War, the British-owned American Marconi Company had been taken over by a new company called the Radio Corporation of America, owned jointly by General Electric and Westinghouse.

In 1915, the company's commercial manager, David Sarnoff, had written a memorandum to management which brought no response. The memo, now regarded as a legend in the communications business, read in part:

"I have in mind a plan of development that would make radio a household utility in the same sense as a piano or phonograph. The idea is to bring music into the home by wireless."

Sarnoff had achieved fame in 1912 as the young wireless operator in New York who heard the distress calls from the liner Titanic after it crashed into an iceberg on its maiden voyage from England to New York.

Following the takeover of the Marconi company, Sarnoff resurrected his visionary memo and sent it to his new bosses, together with a prediction that an investment in "wireless" would generate sales of $80 million within two years. The sceptical company directors appropriated the grand sum of $2,000 for the development of Sarnoff's idea. Between 1922 and 1924, RCA's radio sales amounted to $83 million.

His vision was further demonstrated by another memo he wrote to management, this time in 1923:

"I believe that television, which is the technical name for seeing as well as hearing by radio, will come to pass in the future."

By 1922, there were over three million radio "receiving sets" in operation in Canada and the United States, tuning in to more than 200 broadcasting stations. People in Kitchener and Waterloo enthusiastically bought coils and resistors to make little crystal sets or kits of parts they assembled by following a booklet of instructions. Soon, the squeals of battery-powered two-tube radio sets could be heard all over the neighborhoods.

The *Kitchener Daily Record* sponsored a Radio Club and invited interested people to attend a meeting at the YMCA.

That same year, the term wireless to describe the receiving set was largely discontinued in favor of "radio," at least in North America. In Britain, wireless remained the generic description for decades.

Carl Pollock had been caught up in the radio craze as a student at Berlin High School. He and a friend had experimented with coils, condensers and wire, much of which they begged from Alex Welker at the Victoria Street factory, to make what was known as a cats whisker crystal receiver.

Later, he and Ted Gowan helped Carl Rumpel, son of a prominent Kitchener felt manufacturer, set up an amateur broadcasting station in Rumpel's spacious home, from which they played phonograph records. Just how many people were listening to these budding broadcasters was never recorded. But in time, the station became known by the call letters CJCF and the *Daily Record* sponsored Sunday evening broadcasts of popular music.

A.B. Pollock began to recognize that his son's hobby was more than a passing fad. The newspapers were constantly reporting developments that told him that he had better take a serious interest in the effects of this phenomenon on the phonograph business.

His first tentative step was to get into the flourishing radio parts business with the Music Master, a patented loudspeaker. This consisted of an ornate cabinet made by the Elmira plant, and a mahogany horn which was mounted on a beautiful die-cast base at the Victoria Street plant. Carl Pollock later described it as "a beautiful design— the finest on the market."

But Otto Heineman had bigger ideas. On one of A.B.'s business trips to New York, Heineman told him he should get into the manufacture of radios. Heineman himself had established the General Wireless Corporation of Elyria, Ohio.

Heineman introduced A.B. to David Grimes, who was making a name for himself as a designer of radios. Grimes had invented the Grimes Inverse Duplex, a four-tube radio that used two tubes twice, a great saving on the batteries used to power it.

Grimes agreed to license the Kitchener company to make and sell his radios in Canada. A new Canadian company, the Grimes Radio Corporation, was established. To set up the new operation, A.B. hired Bill Cook, a young engineer recommended by David Grimes.

Cook, a graduate of Tufts College in Boston, had worked for the General Electric Company of New Jersey and the New York Telephone Company before joining Grimes Radio Corp. in New York.

When Cook arrived in Kitchener, he was given a corner of the Victoria Street building—about 500 square feet—in which to manufacture the new line of radios, which were to be incorporated into Phonola cabinets made in Elmira.

His first assistant was John Koegler, who was given the task of making the tooling and fixtures required. The first sample was taken by Bill Cook to show at the Canadian National Exhibition in Toronto, no doubt to measure public response to this new idea in radio. He later recalled that it had "a large tinhorn-type speaker, three dials and three knobs, was operated by batteries and sold for $175, a considerable sum in those days."

The CNE display showed that Pollock had made the right decision. Letters, telegrams and telephone calls poured into the Kitchener office from people clamoring to buy the Grimes Inverse Duplex radio.

An interesting off-shoot of this activity

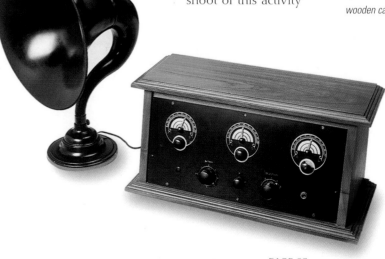

The first Grimes Inverse Duplex radio, made in 1925. The stark design was quickly replaced by furniture-styled wooden cabinets.

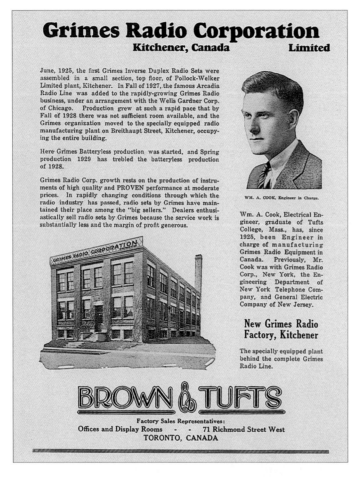

Grimes Radio Corporation
Kitchener, Canada   Limited

June, 1925, the first Grimes Inverse Duplex Radio Sets were assembled in a small section, top floor, of Pollock-Welker Limited plant, Kitchener. In Fall of 1927, the famous Arcadia Radio Line was added to the rapidly-growing Grimes Radio business, under an arrangement with the Wells Gardner Corp. of Chicago. Production grew at such a rapid pace that by Fall of 1928 there was not sufficient room available, and the Grimes organization moved to the specially equipped radio manufacturing plant on Breithaupt Street, Kitchener, occupying the entire building.

Here Grimes Batteryless production was started, and Spring production 1929 has trebled the batteryless production of 1928.

Grimes Radio Corp. growth rests on the production of instruments of high quality and PROVEN performance at moderate prices. In rapidly changing conditions through which the radio industry has passed, radio sets by Grimes have maintained their place among the "big sellers." Dealers enthusiastically sell radio sets by Grimes because the service work is substantially less and the margin of profit generous.

WM. A. COOK, Engineer in Charge.

Wm. A. Cook, Electrical Engineer, graduate of Tufts College, Mass., has, since 1925, been Engineer in charge of manufacturing Grimes Radio Equipment in Canada. Previously, Mr. Cook was with Grimes Radio Corp., New York, the Engineering Department of New York Telephone Company, and General Electric Company of New Jersey.

New Grimes Radio Factory, Kitchener

The specially equipped plant behind the complete Grimes Radio Line.

BROWN & TUFTS

Factory Sales Representatives:
Offices and Display Rooms   -   -   71 Richmond Street West
TORONTO, CANADA

was the development of loudspeakers for outdoor use. John Koegler recalled making the first system used to provide musical accompaniment for skating on the ice in Victoria Park in Kitchener. A similar speaker system was installed at the Kitchener Farmers Market for a carnival organized by the Imperial Order of Daughters of the Empire (IODE), of which Racie Pollock was an active member. But the grandest installation of them all was on the roof of Kitchener-Waterloo Collegiate in Kitchener "in order to broadcast the first concert of the Peace Tower carillon in Ottawa to commemorate Canada's 60th anniversary of Confederation on July 1, 1927."

While this was going on, A.B. Pollock and Otto Heineman were coming to a parting of the ways, for reasons that were not recorded.

It is possible that Heineman, after 10 years in the record-manufacturing and distribution business, had became discouraged with the intense competition and constant feuding that had characterized the industry almost from its start. He obviously decided to abandon his position in the industry and concentrate his resources on phonograph manufacturing and on the rapidly-developing radio business.

This is indicated by an announcement made by the General Phonograph Company that it was discontinuing the manufacture and distribution of the Phonola and Okeh lines, as well as the importation of the Odeon label. The distribution of these records in Canada was turned over to the Phonola Company in Elmira.

Soon afterwards, A.B. and Alex Welker announced the formation of a new company, Pollock-Welker Limited. They bought back their Kitchener plant from General Phonograph, paying $100,000 for the real estate and $43,000 for materials and stock-in-trade. The transaction was recorded in the minutes of the new company's first meeting, held on March 12, 1925.

The Elmira plant, which apparently had not been included in the original takeover by Heineman's company, continued to operate as a separate company.

Now, the two original partners were running three manufacturing concerns: Pollock-Welker Ltd. and Grimes Radio Corporation on Victoria Street in Kitchener and The Phonola Company in Elmira.

Around the time, there was a dramatic development which was to change the direction of the phonograph business forever. Scientists at Western Electric's research department (later Bell Telephone Laboratories) converted sound waves into electrical impulses, amplified the vibrations picked up by the phonograph needle and reproduced a much higher quality of sound than the sound from mechanically-produced vibrations.

The parallel improvement in record quality came at a time when the industry was suffering from the inroads made by radio. The severity of radio's impact is clearly demonstrated by these statistics: Sales of phonographs and records in Canada and the United States went from $59 million in 1921 to $24 million in 1925—a drop of more than 50 percent.

The new development gave phonograph and record manufacturers the opportunity to introduce new products. One company caused a sensation with its all-electrical phonograph. Brunswick Records announced a 12-inch long playing record that—still rotating at 78 rpm—ran for 40 minutes and was capable of reproducing whole symphonies.

In the longer term, the introduction of electrically-powered phonographs and the parallel development of radio led to the design of combination radio-phonographs.

Pollock-Welker Limited took advantage of these developments and introduced its new Phonola at the 1926 Canadian National Exhibition.

Sales of the new Phonola immediately began to improve. Portable phonographs became a hot seller at the same time and the Pollock-Welker "improved" Pulwel portable, which sold for as little as $15, was a popular choice.

The pace of growth enabled the company to proudly announce later that it had gone "from 100 phonographs in 1907 to 10,000 a year in 1928." The financial statements of the Phonola Company for 1928 showed sales of almost $216,000. It was clear that the phonograph business could exist side-by-side with the radio business, despite a pronouncement to the contrary by the great Thomas Edison.

Edison's company had been slow to convert its recordings from the original cylinder format to disc. So it was with more than a little touch of sour grapes that the

Pamphlet promoting three models of the popular Pulwel Portable was aimed at dealers.

renowned inventor said that radio was a fad that had come and gone. His description of radio as "already a back number," was to come back to haunt him.

Eventually Edison's company made the change from recorded cylinders to discs but it was too late. In 1929, the company announced:

"Discontinuance of the making of Edison phonograph records is now announced by Thomas A. Edison Inc. Their record factory will be used for the production of radio."

The pace of development of radio technology became so rapid that manufacturers formed Canadian Radio Patents, an industry organization which made all patents available to any manufacturer on payment of a fee. Grimes Radio Corporation was one of the first to apply for such a manufacturing licence.

This turned out to be a significant development for Pollock-Welker in light of the introduction of radios powered by electricity (AC or alternating current), replacing the original battery-powered versions (DC or direct current).

A U.S. manufacturer of one of these early plug-in models was Wells-Gardner of Chicago. Allen Gardner of the company title wanted to exploit the Canadian market but quickly found that he would have to pay a handsome fee to Canadian Radio Patents, which would have allowed Canadian firms to make his patented electrically-powered product.

The alternative, he discovered, was to find a Canadian manufacturer to make his radios under licence.

As he wandered the streets of downtown Toronto pondering the strange ways of Canadian business, he stopped in front of a retail store displaying a Grimes Inverse Duplex radio made in Kitchener. Knowing the limitations of the Grimes machine and aware that Grimes had not introduced an AC-powered version, he spotted an opportunity.

He called A.B. Pollock in Kitchener and suggested that he import Wells-Gardner electric radios into Canada under the Canadian Radio Patents licence held by Grimes. In return, he offered Wells-Gardner's technical assistance in the development of Pollock's radio business. He told Pollock:

"I think you need Wells-Gardner as much as Wells-Gardner needs you."

Intrigued, A.B. invited Mr. Gardner to Kitchener. It was a move that was to raise sales to new heights.

A.B. and Alex Welker agreed that their Grimes Radio Corporation would pay design fees to the Chicago firm in return for the right to manufacture the Wells-Gardner sets in Kitchener.

The Wells-Gardner firm had quickly built up a large volume of business by making AC-powered radios for large U.S. retailers including J.C. Penney and Montgomery Ward. As a result,

An early model of the Wells-Gardner radio made in Kitchener under the Grimes name.

they were able to buy supplies and components at a much lower cost than Grimes could in Canada. Pollock and Welker were able to take advantage of this buying power.

It was obvious that the small section of the Victoria Street plant used by Bill Cook and his band of assistants was inadequate for the much larger operation that was about to be launched. Up to this point, about 4,000 Grimes radios had been built at the Victoria Street plant with a workforce of only 10 people.

The radio division moved to a three-storey building on nearby Breithaupt Street, previously the Lady Belle shoe plant. John Koegler was sent to the Wells-Gardner plant in Chicago to learn first-hand about manufacturing the batteryless radios. He wrote about the aftermath of his visit:

"As we were the only radio plant in town, no experienced help could be hired. I had to train each and every one of them in the fascinating art of building radios. After the introduction of the superheterodyne, I conducted the first classroom instructions in basic radio and electricity."

Later, he and Carl Pollock would take "some of the boys" to lectures at the Institute of Radio Engineering in Toronto, stopping on the way home for hamburgers and hot dogs at Clappisons Corners.

More salesmen were hired and soon the radio operation employed 40 people.

In the fall of 1929, Carl Pollock had married Helen Isobel Chestnut in St. Catharines, whom he had met while at the University of Toronto.

His interest in radio and electronics had led him first to McMaster University (then located on Bloor Street in Toronto) and then on to the University of Toronto, where he graduated in electrical engineering. While there, he won three special awards for high standing, including a bronze medal awarded by the British Association for the Advancement of Science. He crowned his academic career by becoming one of two students to be awarded a Massey Foundation fellowship for two years of study at Oxford University.

Carl Pollock and his bride-to-be, Helen Chestnut, photographed in 1926.

The *Kitchener Daily Record's* account of the award said:

"As is often found in brilliant scholars, Carl is also a formidable athlete. He holds records for the mile run and the 500-yard dash and has won the coveted 'T' three times."

Helen had stayed in Canada when Carl sailed from Montreal on September 17, 1926, bound for England. He read physics at Magdalen College, and was intrigued by the prospect of an academic career. When he returned from Oxford, he was hired as a teaching assistant working on wind tunnel research at the University of Toronto.

Carl Pollock, an outstanding student, became a Massey Fellow at Oxford University.

NEW SCHOLARSHIP FOR CARL POLLOCK

Local Young Man Awarded Fellowship Course At Oxford University By Massey Foundation

Following their marriage, he and Helen lived in Toronto but the challenges and opportunities offered by the family business put an end to any ambitions of becoming a university professor. They moved to Kitchener and Carl went to work for his father.

He started in earnest to learn about every aspect of the business, particularly the manufacture of radios. He helped set up test equipment in the new radio plant and worked in the metal working shop. From January to June of 1930, he delved into the mysteries of retailing by working in the office of Brown and Tufts, the company's Toronto sales agents.

In July, his father appointed him manager of the Grimes Radio Corporation. The employees avoided the confusion of addressing two Mr. Pollocks by calling the father and son team "A.B." and "C.A." Carl rolled up his sleeves and put his considerable energy into making Grimes Radio a success.

Thousands of radios were turned out at the Breithaupt Street plant. More than two-thirds of the units sold bore the names of major retailers such as Eatons, Simpsons and the Hudson Bay Company and these "private brands" were given priority. To keep these major customers happy, Grimes developed a distinctive appearance for each one, so that they were not all selling the same radio with a different name attached.

On other sets, the Grimes name was replaced by Phonola. There were dozens of different cabinet styles to suit the public's wide-ranging taste but underneath the polished wooden surface, the chassis bore the Wells-Gardner imprint.

Increased sales of radios meant more business for the two associated companies. The Pollock-Welker plant made more parts for the radio department than it ever had for its original phonograph products. The Phonola plant in Elmira couldn't keep up with the demand for radio cabinets and had to have some made by a Kitchener furniture manufacturer.

C.A. Pollock later recalled that the three companies controlled by his father employed only about 150 people in 1929 and had combined sales of about $300,000. The company's prosperity was evident when $5 gold pieces were awarded as prizes for races held at the annual picnic. Parties were held at Hallowe'en and Christmas and C.A. handed out boxes of chocolates to everyone.

But trouble was just around the corner. In the aftermath of the First World War, Canada's economy had ridden a roller coaster—up one year and down the next. South of the border, the "Roaring Twenties" had given the world bathtub gin, flappers and silent movie stars. Canadians had to endure a post-war downturn that didn't really disappear until 1924. But then came an explosive spurt of growth.

Canadians flocked to buy a Model T Ford for $595.

Output tripled to more than 188,000 vehicles a year and Canada became the world's second-largest exporter of cars and parts, after the United States.

The burgeoning pace continued during the second half of the 1920s. *Canadian Business* magazine described the mood: "Almost everywhere you looked, the signs were favorable. Domestic construction seemed to be thriving, thanks to a housing boom. Most people, especially in Ontario's thriving factories, would have assumed they were well on their way to Nirvana. Employment levels rose—real wages were rising and coincident with a burst of growth in retailing, more and better consumer goods became available."

It was aboard this surge of growth that the three Pollock-controlled enterprises looked forward to the 1930s.

But the stock market crash of October 1929 sent shock waves rippling outwards. Almost nobody was left unscathed by the Great Depression that followed. "The Hungry Thirties"..."The Dirty Thirties"—whatever the label—the euphoria induced by a seemingly unending pattern of expansion and growth vanished overnight.

Kitchener's furniture industry was hit hard. Sales fell from $11 million in 1929 to $1 million in 1932. Unemployment rolls swelled beyond imagination. Kitchener recorded 4,434 people on welfare at the lowest point of the "seven lean years," as they came to be known.

The Board of Trade campaigned for government-guaranteed bank loans for the owners of "24 factories in this locality alone which are inoperative as well as a number of others barely existing." The pleas fell on deaf ears.

By 1931, A.B. Pollock's businesses were among those described as "barely existing."

It must have seemed ironic to him that hard times had followed so quickly on the heels of what had appeared to be an exciting period of growth ahead. Urged on by his son, C.A., he had agreed to replace the Wells-Gardner designed radios with sets engineered and manufactured by their own employees at the Breithaupt Street plant.

The decision had been influenced by the increasing demands of their larger customers for faster deliveries. The new radio engineering department had only just started into production when the Depression caught up with them.

It came in the form of cancelled orders from the same retail chains who had been so demanding a few months earlier. Eatons, Simpsons and Hudson Bay were among the major customers who had experienced a severe drop in sales as people afraid of losing their jobs and their homes stopped buying such luxuries as radios and phonographs.

The company was left with a large inventory of finished products and the materials to make more—its resources tied up in assets that could not be turned into cash.

Ed Schaub, the Elmira plant superintendent, later recalled those dreadful days:

"Things got pretty tough. We were off work so much, Chunker (Clayton) Allgeier and I had nothing to do. We were told we could go out and sell radios so we could get just enough money to keep living."

Ed Schaub (left) and "Chunker" Allgeier were the only two employees left at the Depression-hit woodworking plant in Elmira.

There was no record of how successful these two reluctant salesmen were but another comment by Ed Schaub was revealing: "One year (during the Depression) we made only 2,400 cabinets and A.B. said he could have gone out and bought them cheaper. We were off half the time and were quite happy to just make them."

John Koegler had similar recollections: "Things got tougher and tougher. Radio production lasted only a few months. Thousands of workers in the area were out of work. For a long period, only a few employees remained on duty. Others were thankful to even get 11 hours in a week. No other work was available."

The metal working plant's production of small windup motors was faring just as badly and struggling to stay in business.

Then came the hardest blow of all.

The stress of coping with the recession became too much for A.B. Pollock, who was then in his mid-fifties. He suffered a heart attack and was ordered by his doctor to stay away from the business and all its worries.

It isn't difficult to imagine the agonies A.B. endured in accepting this decree.

Purchase of this plant on Edward St. (later renamed Duke St.) in Kitchener enabled the company to move its furniture and woodworking operations from Elmira. After adding the radio and communications division and head office operations, it became known as Plant 1.

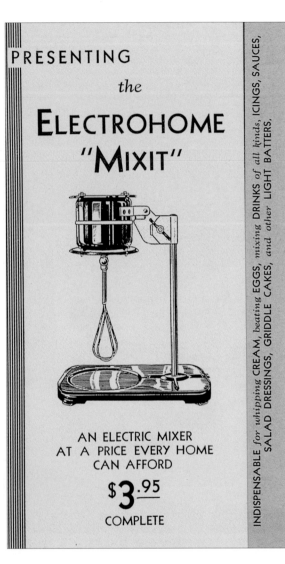

PRESENTING

the

ELECTROHOME
"MIXIT"

AN ELECTRIC MIXER
AT A PRICE EVERY HOME
CAN AFFORD

$3.95

COMPLETE

INDISPENSABLE *for whipping* CREAM, *beating* EGGS, *mixing* DRINKS *of all kinds,* ICINGS, SAUCES, SALAD DRESSINGS, GRIDDLE CAKES, *and other* LIGHT BATTERS.

Electrohome Fans

Cool as a Sea Breeze

Electrohome
PORTABLE AIR CONDITIONER

THE MODERN WAY TO HEALTH AND COMFORT

THE ALPINE MODEL

Metal cabinet in durable and attractive light brown ripple finish. Tank capacity of 3¼ gallons, and air capacity of 9000 cubic feet per hour. Equipped with silent Electrohome motor and 8″ fan; 3 washable filters. Ideal for small apartments and offices. 15¾″ wide, 11¼″ deep, and 19″ high. Price complete, ready to plug in. $32.50.

CHAPTER FOUR

1933-1945 The Next Generation Takes Over

The Electrohome name, introduced in 1933, became widely known with the introduction of food mixers, fans and humidifiers (at left). Department stores ordered them with their own brand name and designs, such as the Viking line for Eatons (above right).

"One million dollars! You mean we sold a million dollars-worth?"

Carl Pollock smiled at his father. "It's hard to imagine after all we've been through."

But it was true. It was now 1938 and the Depression seemed to be over. Thanks in great part to the efforts of Carl Pollock, the family enterprise had overcome the biggest challenge in its history.

During the five previous years, the three businesses had been consolidated and Arthur Pollock's long-time business partner, Alex Welker, had departed.

A.B., apparently recovered from the effects of his heart attack, had good reason to be grateful that Carl had opted for a business career instead of pursuing his earlier goal of becoming a university professor.

When Carl Pollock stepped into the breach to take over the management of the company during his father's convalescence, he was able for the first time to form a clear picture of the company in its entirety. He saw the interchange of activities between the three manufacturing concerns. The Phonola Company, for example, was building cabinets for the Grimes Radio line; Pollock-Welker built the mechanisms for Phonola gramophones, and so on.

He also saw how badly the company had been hurt by the loss of orders from the major retailing chains and he vowed never again to be put in a position where major customers could decide the company's fate. A new policy was adopted which limited the amount of private label manufacturing to 25 per cent of goods under manufacture at any one time. Later events were to show that it was impossible to uphold this policy.

C.A. was a man who kept abreast of new technological advances in the rapidly-changing field of home entertainment.

Inventors on both sides of the Atlantic had been experimenting for several years with television or radio-movies as this development was sometimes called. As early as 1926, John Logie Baird, a Scotsman, and Charles Francis Jenkins, an American, had shown the first live pictures for audiences in department stores, at trade fairs and at exhibitions.

Canadians could watch demonstrations in the early 1930s at department stores in Toronto, Montreal and Winnipeg. Foster Hewitt, the "voice of hockey", was the master of ceremonies for Western Television's display at Eatons in Toronto. In 1931, Ted Rogers was granted a licence to broadcast experimental television from his Toronto radio station. His son, also named Ted, later became a powerful figure in Canadian broadcasting and cable TV.

In the midst of these exciting developments, Carl Pollock was busy instituting change himself. He persuaded his father to combine the three business operations into one company, with a central management structure providing overall direction. It was a strategy that provided another example of his energy, vision and intuition.

The new organization was named Dominion

Electrohome Industries Limited. For C.A., the name choice seemed to fall into the same pattern as A.B.'s coin toss. Suggested names for the company were written on scraps of paper and placed in a hat. The first name drawn was the one suggested by C.A.

The company came into being in April 1933 with the purchase of the combined assets of Pollock-Welker Ltd. and Grimes Radio Corporation Ltd., valued at $495,838.76. The directors were A.B. Pollock, C.A. Pollock, Alex Welker, A.G. Farrow, an independent sales representative; C.L. Rason, a local accountant and auditor; C.C. Dewey, a Kitchener stockbroker; and K.A.A. Loth, a female office clerk who acted as board secretary.

There were also a number of shareholders listed— among them several women—which was the first indication that A.B. had raised operating capital by selling shares. One of the shareholders was Frederick G. Gardiner who went on to become the first chairman of

The consolidation of the company's businesses is reflected in these old and new letterhead samples.

the Metropolitan Toronto Council. A year later, the board was reduced in size and consisted of A.B. Pollock, Carl Pollock and Alex Welker, together with Harold Fry of Fry and Co., Toronto stockbrokers (later Burns Fry).

Management responsibilities were divided more clearly, an acknowledgement of the different styles of father and son. Carl became general manager and took on responsibility for both Grimes Radio Corporation and the Phonola and furniture operation in Elmira. He shared an office with his father, who, while involved in the overall direction of the company, concentrated on overseeing the motor and metal products division on Victoria Street.

Even though the Depression was over, sales continued at a low level. As a cost-cutting measure, it was decided to move the radio manufacturing operation from Breithaupt Street back to its original Victoria Street location.

Slowly, however, public confidence improved. In the United States, President Franklin Delano Roosevelt's "New Deal" had begun to fuel the economy. People started to buy consumer goods again which was reflected in improved share prices on the Toronto Stock Exchange.

The effect for Electrohome was an increasing level of orders from such customers as Eatons and Simpsons, particularly for radios. A building on Duke Street West in Kitchener was acquired to give the radio division more space. By November 1935, radio production had reached new heights—over 100 sets a day. There were 128 people on the company's payroll.

Car radio sales were steadily increasing. Using Wells-Gardner designs, the company took advantage of buoyant demand and it wasn't long before car radios were making a significant contribution to Electrohome's sales figures.

In 1935, the partnership between A.B. Pollock and Alex Welker came to an end. There are no recorded details of the reason for this parting of the ways. Donald Sykes, former executive vice-president and board chairman, believes Welker left because he found mass manufacturing limiting and that he felt his skills were not being used. After 28 years with the organization he helped establish, he set up a new business, Welker Industries Ltd. in an old cooperage building on Regina Street in Waterloo and started making health vibrators.

By this time, Carl Pollock and his wife, Helen, were the proud parents of a daughter, Barbara, born in 1933. They lived on Ahrens Street, off Queen Street North in downtown Kitchener. In January 1936, a son, John, was born.

The pace of business quickened and so did the rate of change at Electrohome. To ensure close communication

Consumer demand for car radios contributed to improving sales figures.

between the manufacturing operations, the Phonola operation was moved to Kitchener. One story about this tells of Arthur Pollock passing an empty furniture factory on Edward Street (later Duke Street) in Kitchener every day on his way to the Phonola plant in Elmira. One day while driving past the place with C.A., he is reported to have said: "Why don't we buy this place so I won't have to run back and forth to Elmira?"

Whatever the reasoning, the large four-storey factory (formerly the Malcolm and Hill furniture plant) was bought for only $26,000 and converted for use by what was to become the furniture and woodworking division. Up to this point, the Elmira woodworking operation had existed solely to manufacture Phonola phonograph cabinets as well as cabinets for the Grimes radio models. The seasonal nature of this business would leave the factory idle once orders had been filled and despatched to retail stores across the country. To keep the staff busy, the company had from time to time made occasional tables.

But with the move to Edward Street, Carl saw an opportunity to make a serious entry into furniture manufacturing. It was to be a move with long-term repercussions. The new business grew to become a major contributor to company revenue for many years.

Carl Pollock came up with a name for the furniture line, Deilcraft, which was based on the first four letters of the company's corporate name. It was to become a household name in the Canadian home furnishings industry, symbolic of fine quality Canadian furniture. In fact, the company traded on this reputation by featuring "Cabinets by Deilcraft" in promoting home entertainment products.

The Imperial Furniture Company of Grand Rapids, Michigan, licensed Electrohome to manufacture and sell a line of tables in Canada under the name of Deilcraft Imperial. The relationship lasted for many years.

The company's entry into the furniture business "took the country by storm," according to a 1947 edition of the company newsletter, *Sparks and Chips*, commemorating Electrohome's 40th anniversary. It said:

"Dominion Electrohome Industries Limited rose overnight from a comparatively obscure position in the furniture industry to one of equal importance with the largest and most outstanding furniture manufacturers in Canada.

"Within a few weeks the name Deilcraft had become famous as representing the finest type of occasional furniture ever produced in Canada.

"Today, over 450 stores from New Westminster, B.C. to Glace Bay, N.S. are featuring Electrohome furniture. Millions of people are reading the Deilcraft story in the best magazines and periodicals in this country. Public demand is

The introduction
of the Deilcraft
name signalled the
company's entry into
furniture-making.
Electrohome
eventually became
one of Canada's
largest furniture
manufacturers.

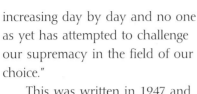

Occasional tables were first made to keep the factory busy between orders for phonograph and radio cabinets.

increasing day by day and no one as yet has attempted to challenge our supremacy in the field of our choice."

This was written in 1947 and showed the rapid acceptance of the Deilcraft name, in the 10 years following its introduction.

The Edward Street factory was too large for just the furniture and woodworking operation and it was decided to make use of the excess space by moving sales, accounting and the main business office there. The Edward Street location became Plant 1 and Victoria Street became Plant 2 and was named the Appliances and Metal Products division.

The seasonal pattern of radio and phonograph sales, which peaked in late summer and early fall, led A.B. and C.A. Pollock into another new business. While the Deilcraft furniture line proved successful in keeping the woodworking plant busy, a similar problem existed with radio and phonograph production. The solution was found in the small electric motors used in phonographs.

Electrically-powered phonographs were a natural evolution in the development and use of electrical audio amplification. As was to happen in so many other areas of developing technology, the company led the way in Canada in introducing sub-fractional horsepower electrical motors to power the phonograph turntable,

which replaced the renowned Helycon spring-wound mechanism. A.B. tracked down a U.S. company which specialized in motors used for air moving appliances, the Universal Electric Company in Owasso, Mich. The owners, the Hoddie brothers, agreed to licence Pollock-Welker to make their designs.

The first such motor was made in 1930. Old meeting notes recorded the decision "to make one hundred 60-cycle and one hundred 25-cycle electric motors" to drive turntables for radio-phono combinations built in the radio plant.

The opportunities for other uses of these motors caught the imagination of the two Pollocks.

"Why not use the same motors and make fans?" asked A.B., recognizing a product which was well within the capabilities of the Victoria Street plant.

The result was the introduction of electric fans for summer use and a short time later, the invention of the humidifier for winter use in the dry, heated homes of Canadians. Both products were subsequently made at the metal products factory, filling in the gaps of seasonal radio and phonograph production.

The company eventually became the biggest manufacturer of fans in Canada. The original models were painted black and were all one design. Then color choices were introduced— blue and beige, for example—and features added.

The company was constantly searching for new products. Cigarette vending machines and refrigerators were among those actively considered.

One successful search by Carl Pollock led to a new

THE *Electrohome*
"Breeze Spreader"

Spreads
Cool
Comfort
Without
a Blast

Everyone within the wide range of a "Breeze-Spreader" Fan benefits from the "No-draft" air distribution — a safe, steady, comfortable breeze over 70% greater area than with ordinary fans. The greatest advance in fan performance since the invention of the Oscillator.

Even when oscillating ordinary fans cool only one person at a time with a blast.

"Breeze-Spreader" Fans distribute safe, refreshing comfort over wide area—without drafts.

AVAILABLE IN TWO MODELS

10" STRAIGHT   { 25 Cycle—Model 1102SB
BLOW   { 60 Cycle—Model 1106SB

Heavy "Tear Drop" cast base adjustable for wall mounting if desired. Large size, quiet running "In-Duc-To" Motor with switch. Louvres adjustable to increase or decrease breeze spread. Rich ebony black finish with cadmium guard.

10" OSCILLATING   { 25 Cycle—Model 11020B
{ 60 Cycle—Model 11060B

All the features of the Straight Blow Model, plus oscillating movement governed by light pressure, positive control. Pleasing streamlined design with "Bullet Nose" Motor case and polished Chrome Hub cap.

"*Breeze Spread*" IS AN EXCLUSIVE ELECTROHOME FEATURE

"Breeze spreader" fan had vanes to direct air in different directions, a forerunner of fans with an oscillating mechanism.

An early humidifier (1933).

design for humidifiers for home and office use which he patented in 1937.

The company wanted to describe the new product as an air conditioner because it circulated, filtered and cleaned the air. But a Canadian government ruling decreed that unless the machines cooled the air as well, they could not be called air conditioners. The product was widely sold in Canada—it had no competition for many years—and its name, the Humidaire, became a generic term for humidifiers.

The driving force behind the company's expansion of both its product line and its distribution network was J. Gordon Tufts. Originally a partner in a Toronto sales agency which represented the company, he had joined the company as a full-time employee after his agency was forced out of business by the Depression.

A.B. hired him in 1934 to take charge of private brand label sales, which became his specialty. He was made a member of the board of directors and his energy and vision influenced the course of the company's business for many years.

Minutes of the board of directors fixed his remuneration in 1936 at $100 per week plus a half per cent commission on radio sales. He was also provided with a Chevrolet coupe, "purchased by the company for $500 for company business."

Tufts enjoyed the same level of pay as both A.B. and C.A. Pollock at this time. The salary levels reflected the improving state of the company. In 1933, A.B. had drawn only $40 a week and C.A. was paid $65. By 1936, the company could afford $100 a week for both Pollocks and Tufts. The directors' minutes recorded a vote of thanks to A.B. for "his untiring efforts to help the company during the recent strenuous years," noting how his associates had appreciated "his cooperation in keeping his own remuneration to a very low level."

The increased level of business enabled the company to pay a five percent raise to all factory employees effective January 1, 1937. Bonuses were paid to senior executives: A.B. received $1,500 and C.A. $2,500. The super-

intendent of the radio division, W.D. Nesbitt, received a bonus of $125 on top of his weekly salary of $65.

In April 1937, A.D. Coltman was hired as sales representative for western Canada, at $75 a week plus commission. He had worked for the Hudson Bay Company and knew the western retail business intimately. His office expense was estimated at $8,000 a year.

C.A.'s position as general manager brought him into regular contact with employees. In 1937, he instigated the formation of an Employees Welfare Committee which resulted in the introduction of a group insurance plan and the provision of tennis courts for employees.

A.B. had long encouraged the participation of employees in sports activities. Harvey Durst, who was hired in 1937 at age 17 as an office boy recalled in a 1984 interview how Electrohome had sponsored employee teams in local bowling, hockey and baseball leagues.

"We had one of the best ball teams in the city. We won the senior championship twice and A.B. threw a party for us at the Conestoga Hotel. We were the best-dressed team in the league. We didn't have to wear our own clothes—we had grey trousers and shirts with the company insignia on the back."

Durst, who was paid $6 a week to start, went on to work for many years in costing and the materials department. He said the sports activities kept up morale and fostered a team spirit that carried over into the plant during working hours. "If you fell behind in your job,

a couple of guys would always come and help you out."

He told of A.B. attending hockey games to watch company-sponsored teams. "He would sit there wrapped in a blanket and the next day, he'd tell you if he felt you had too many penalties."

This same team spirit was evident when customers demanded something out of the ordinary. Gordon Fowler, who started in sales in the Toronto office in 1937, remembered an occasion when Eatons came to Electrohome with an order for 20,000 mantel radios they wanted to sell for $14.98. To get the order, the employees agreed to take a pay cut of 2-3 cents an hour. The alternative was to close the plant for a few days, said Fowler.

Despite Electrohome's improving fortunes, the company operated on a somewhat hand-to-mouth basis in the period leading up to 1939. Gordon Fowler recalled receiving a call almost every week from Les Hope, the company treasurer. "He wanted me to go over to the Eatons office to pick up a cheque (he remembered one amount being for $14,000). He said we needed it to make the payroll."

Agnes Ellert, who started in the office in 1931 and worked for Electrohome for 46 years, told another story which underlined the seasonal nature of the business, a result of the company's reliance on department store orders.

"Around 1938, there were slack periods when people were sent home for a month and then get called back. There was one time when the plant would shut down just before Christmas and wouldn't start up again until April."

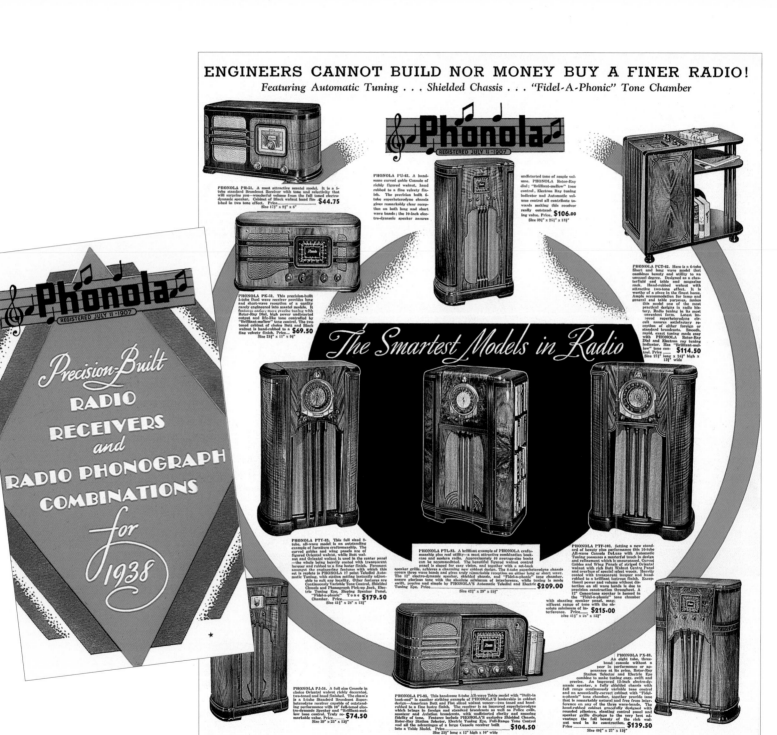

This 1938 product catalogue featured many different models and styles of radios.

Despite the slack periods, the financial statement for the year which ended April 30, 1938, showed sales of all products totalled $1,005,442.64. Achieving sales of over a million dollars was a remarkable turnaround from the bleak days of the Depression and indicated the importance of the radio market.

Radio sales accounted for $848,884 of the total. Sales of other products were abysmal by comparison: Humidifiers, just over $64,000; furniture cabinets, close to $60,000; and phonographs and record players, $2,096. Fan sales were listed at a mere $58.47.

Despite C.A.'s vow of limiting sales of private brand products to 25 per cent of total production, it was evident that sales of private label products were the lifeblood of the business during this period.

Thanks largely to the efforts of Gordon Tufts, most of the company's output of phonographs and radios went to the major retail chains in Canada. They bore such names as Viking and Minerva (Eatons), Dictator (Hudson Bay Co.) and Serenader (Simpsons). Car radios and furniture, fans and humidifiers were also made under private label. As a result, there were times that the production lines were so busy making products to be sold under another name that there was little time to make the company's own name brands.

The outbreak of war in 1939 was to have a profound effect on Electrohome. The million dollar sales figure became just a tidemark on the wall of history as defence contracts for all three manufacturing plants created new levels from which to measure achievements. Sales for all three divisions rose in 1940 to $1,117, 200 with a gross

profit of $246,565; in 1941 to $1,372,732; and in 1942 to $2,315,248.

The furniture and woodworking division discontinued all standard lines of furniture to manufacture a range of products required for many aspects of the war effort.

The men who worked at Edward Street applied their skills to make wooden aircraft components which required the kind of precision and attention to detail previously lavished on occasional tables and beautifully-finished cabinets for phonographs and radios.

Thousands of Allied pilots were taught in Cornell Trainers containing parts made in Kitchener by Electrohome craftsmen. The Cornell was used extensively in the Commonwealth air training plan and by U.S. forces.

The company newsletter, *Sparks and Chips*, which came into being in 1942, published a list of the wartime components made by the furniture and woodworking

Wings, tail sections and other parts for the Cornell Trainer were made at the company's woodworking plant during the Second World War.

Further Support to Our Fighting Forces

RADIO AND COMMUNICATIONS DIVISION

Within this Division, complete engineering laboratories and production lines promote with untiring effort the intricate task of supplying Transmitters, Inter-Communication Units and Radio Accessories to the training and fighting forces of the United Nations.

WOODWORKING DIVISION

The home of "Deilcraft" Fine Furniture, now devoted entirely to the production of Wood Aircraft Components—Spars, Fins, Stabilizers and Pilot Seats have taken the place of cabinets and fine furniture on the production lines of this Division.

THE DOMINION ELECTROHOME INDUSTRIES LIMITED   KITCHENER, ONTARIO

Wartime information pamphlet describes the major contributions made by the company.

division. This was after the war had ended and wartime secrecy regulations were no longer in effect. The list showed that 1,004 pairs of wings and 8,000 fins were the biggest item made for the Cornell Trainer. Other components made included centre sections 1,170; stabilizers 1,750; seats, 3,740; and fuselage fairings, 300.

Other products made at the Edward Street factory included cases for mortar sights, artillery boards, map boards and items for truck and ground communication systems such as aerial reels and bases and numerous carrying cases.

Over on Victoria Street, the metal products division spent the war years making various kinds of munitions components including millions of shell exploders. The plant had to be re-equipped to handle the orders for brass magazines, fuse caps, transmitter parts, aircraft seat parts and a number of screw machine parts for other defence contractors.

The production capacity of the plant was almost tripled with the addition of automatic screw machines, punch presses, annealing furnaces and painting and assembling equipment.

The radio division was slower to get into war work. Early defence contracts went mainly to three large companies in Montreal. Electrohome—with a staff of about 150—continued to make domestic radios until 1942. Then things changed quickly.

An order from Research Enterprises Ltd. of Toronto was the first of a series of contracts for communication equipment items that included headsets, aircraft intercom amplifiers, control boxes and the "Number 43 Transmitter,"

for which all production design work was completed by Electrohome engineers. The engineering department was consolidated at the Edward Street plant and extra staff taken on to handle wartime contracts for development work on numerous pieces of "wireless" equipment and components.

During the latter half of the war, the company made staff car radio sets, transceivers for lighthouses watching for submarines along the St. Lawrence, turret assemblies for navy radio receivers, Red Cross radio sets and a vast number of components for installation kits for the "Number 19 Wireless Set," which was carried by troops in the field and was part of the standard equipment for Jeeps.

Shell exploders and fuse caps were among munitions components made at the Victoria Street metal products plant.

Victory bond sales were promoted as part of this display showing wartime products being made by Dominion Electrohome.

The war years brought numerous other changes.

In 1941, C.A. Pollock started the "Good Service Committee," with the intention of making working conditions attractive for employees. Two years later, it was renamed The Electrohome Recreation Association and was made up of members elected from each department. A *Sparks and Chips* article reported:

"During the war years this committee carried on excellent work, not only providing recreation for the members of DEI but providing cigarettes and boxes of goodies for the boys overseas in the armed forces.

"Movie hops were introduced, at which films were shown, followed by dancing. The dances and sports have been well supported by all members. The event of the season is a family picnic held each summer. The sports, the band, the contests and the famous spare ribs supper, followed in the evening by a dance, are talked about for months after the summer is passed."

Sparks and Chips was itself an innovation, again instigated by Carl Pollock "to foster inter-employee relations as well as management-employee relations." When the first issue appeared on December 18, 1942, he was its first editor. The name was suggested by John Koegler in a contest among employees.

Another employee relations innovation was a Long Service Recognition Plan "to recognize and honor members who have served the company loyally and well for ten or more years." A gold pin was awarded to employees reaching their 10th year of service and those with 25 years of service became members of the Quarter Century Club and received a gold watch.

A more significant development in the employee relations area was the establishment of a union in 1943. Factory workers formed the Amalgamated Workers Union which became affiliated not with the larger more powerful U.S.-based labor organizations as was a common practice, but with the Amalgamated Unions of Canada, based in Trail, B.C.

The union executive met monthly with management and relations were reported to be cordial—a situation that was not always the case in later years.

The purchasing department, established in 1936 to centralize this function, grew from two to thirteen people

The company's newsletter was introduced in 1942. The name represented the company's involvement in electrical manufacturing and woodworking.

due to the increasing number of items which had to be bought as the range of products and sales grew. Wartime regulations brought an increase in paperwork and supply difficulties, as told in this account of the time:

"One person spent full time visiting suppliers' plants expediting materials. It was often necessary to travel among rural hardware stores in order to obtain essential small tools such as pliers, files, screwdrivers, etc.

"It was also necessary to visit the Priorities Board in Ottawa and fight for the required priority in order to obtain delivery of materials when needed."

As the Second World War came to a close in 1945, Electrohome ranked as a nationally-known and important company. From a work force of fewer than 400 people before the war, it now employed close to 1,400 in three areas of manufacturing that stood to benefit from the increase in demand for consumer goods that was expected to accompany the return of Canadian forces from far-flung theatres of war.

Many of the men and women who had served their country returned to work at Electrohome, displacing some of the people who had been hired to handle the demands of wartime production.

They joined a company which had acquired new equipment, more production capacity and a wider range of skills. Perhaps more than anything, Electrohome had acquired a new attitude which would make the company a major influence in home furnishings and would provide new opportunities in the home entertainment business.

Production capacity at the Victoria Street plant was tripled with the addition of equipment to meet wartime demands.

CHAPTER FIVE

1946-1954 Postwar Growth

C.A. Pollock was a partner in CKCO-TV, which went on the air in Kitchener in 1954. Coverage of local events, such as this ballgame from Victoria Park, was emphasized from the start.

Small electric motors (above right) found new export markets.

"This is CFCA-FM Radio, serving Kitchener-Waterloo and surrounding communities."

It was 7 p.m. on April 26, 1949, and the sound of the announcer's voice meant that Carl Pollock had finally achieved one of his long-cherished dreams—owning his own radio station.

It was also Canada's first exclusively-FM (frequency modulation) station, a distinction perhaps not appreciated by people passing by the Medical Arts Building on King Street in Kitchener, who may not have noticed the basement location of the new endeavor. They were likely to be more aware of the 250-foot-high transmitter tower built on Baden Hill, which became a landmark for miles around.

The launching of the radio station was just one of a series of developments in the period immediately following the end of the war.

Unprecedented change was about to sweep across Canada—and the world—as men and women returned home after six long years of wearying warfare. They were not immediately aware of the impact they would have on their own and future generations as they returned to their jobs, got married and started raising families. The resulting population increase, eventually labelled The Baby Boom, was to have a profound effect on the lives of everyone.

Electrohome workers celebrated the end of the war with a picnic in Waterloo Park. There was a parade featuring the Electrohome brass band, followed by races, bingo games, pony rides and a softball tournament. The celebration concluded with a dance in the park pavilion with music by Electrohome employee Carl Jantzi and his eight-piece band.

Now it was time to gear up for a peacetime economy. There was a general feeling of optimism as everyone looked forward to a resumption of production to meet the wave of consumer demand that could be expected. People would be shopping for radios, for fans and humidifiers, for furniture—all products made by Electrohome. Or so the feeling went.

But the bonanza did not materialize as soon as expected. Government contracts for wartime products, worth close to $5 million in 1944, were cut in half and then to nothing. The payroll dropped from a peak of 1,393 in July 1943 to 510 in 1945.

Although wartime contracts had brought substantial increases in revenue, the cost of gearing up for them had made serious inroads into working capital. Profits were almost non-existent because of government controls designed to prevent profiteering.

The company needed cash to gear up for the expected postwar boom. One of the first tasks was to convert the two plants from wartime production. The company waged an unsuccessful battle with federal bureaucrats in Ottawa trying to recover some of the cost of repairing and replacing the floors of the Edward Street plant, which company officials pointed out were damaged as a result of wartime manufacturing.

The sorry state of the company's finances is reflected in the minutes of directors' meetings from late 1945 to early 1946. After discussing a possible bond issue to reduce bank loans, the board arranged a $300,000 mortgage at 4%, redeemable through 1958. This was followed in January 1946 with a public issue of $100,000 in common shares, sold on the Toronto Stock Exchange. The issue was arranged and under-written by Fry and Company. Harold Fry's experience and contacts were to prove invaluable during his many years of service as a director.

A wartime ban on the manufacture of consumer radios was lifted and the first peacetime radios came off the production line in December 1945. By March 1946, the economy had begun to pick up and orders were flowing in as wage-earning Canadians ordered radios by the thousands. Even those who lived in remote areas without electricity—northern Quebec, northern Ontario and parts of western Canada—wanted battery-powered radios made by Electrohome.

The Deilcraft Furniture division advertised in leading Canadian consumer magazines and worked hard to rebuild its pre-war dealer network.

By the spring of 1946, according to a *Sparks and Chips* article, "furniture was flowing out of our factory in greater volume than at any time in the history of the company."

The first postwar radio was made in December in 1945. Soon afterwards the company was producing a host of new products including this 1946 radio-phonograph combination.

Deilcraft furniture was greeted enthusiastically as postwar demand increased. Furniture flowed out of the factory "in greater volume than at any time in the company's history."

By the end of 1946, sales had climbed to $1,223,805, but at some cost to A.B. Pollock.

The mortgage bond and the share issue obviously did not provide sufficient cash to get the company through the transition to postwar consumer goods production. On May 22, 1946, The Royal Bank warned the company that it had reached the limit of its line of credit. The bank made it clear that new equity must be found.

The financial deadlock was solved by A.B., who injected the required funds to carry the company through the summer of 1946. It was by no means the last time the company would face a financial crisis.

Despite having to deal with cash flow problems, C.A. Pollock found the time to serve as the 1946 president of the Kitchener Chamber of Commerce and the Ontario Associated Boards of Trade and Chambers of Commerce. He undertook an extensive series of speaking engagements which gave him the opportunity to express his vision of the future for Canada.

He spoke of the need for a new immigration policy so that the country could accommodate "the many Europeans who will want to move to Canada, considering the problems that will be left in Europe."

In Ottawa, he spoke about preserving the free enterprise system. Business people must improve their standard of business ethics, he said. "We must recognize that in operating a business we are setting a standard by which our system will be judged."

He said "the recent trend of unionism is here to stay" and said better industrial relations could be achieved by union-management co-operation.

This philosophy was reflected in Carl Pollock's management style. He was a strong supporter of the Recreation Association and the Long Service Recognition Plan. He re-organized the personnel function into the Industrial Relations Department which administered a group life and health insurance plan, a suggestion plan, safety, health services, training, plant music and canteen services.

Electrohome employees could participate in the company's successes through an incentive plan which enabled workers to earn extra income, known as "co-operative dividends," for extra effort.

And while employees were represented by The Amalgamated Workers Union, the company's labor policy was clearly stated:

"It shall be the Company's constant endeavour to treat the men and women in its employ fairly and in good faith. Every effort will be made, through training and leadership, to develop and utilize to the full each individual's skill and ability. It is the Company's belief that, only by bringing out the best efforts of each member, can the company be assured of success and can the men and women, who carry out the work of

Clayton "Chunker" Allgeier, appointed works manager, 1947.

Queen Street South auditorium, later destroyed by fire, was the scene of "the largest birthday dinner ever held under one roof."

the company, feel satisfied and secure."

In April 1947, Clayton "Chunker" Allgeier was appointed works manager, signalling a major re-organization of the company's management structure.

Chunker Allgeier was hired by the Phonola Company in Elmira as an office boy in 1919. He worked in stock-keeping and shipping before moving to the cost department. He became office manager and in 1943 was made coordinator of the furniture and woodworking division. He later became vice-president of the Deilcraft division and a director of the company. An edition of *Sparks and Chips* which announced his appointment said: "He has gained his popularity by his fair dealings, genial disposition and willingness to help everyone with whom he comes in contact."

Allgeier's new job was to co-ordinate the activities of the three production divisions (furniture and wood-working, appliances and metal products, and radio and communications) and to provide a central contact with sales and service departments.

The re-structuring announcement said it was necessary because of the growing diversity of the company's products and the increasing size of the production divisions.

In 1947, the company celebrated its 40th anniversary with "the largest birthday dinner ever held under one roof." About 650 employees sat

down to dinner in the auditorium on Queen Street in downtown Kitchener (later destroyed by fire). It was also the occasion of A.B. Pollock's 70th birthday and naturally, the company founder was the centre of attention, even though by this time he had very little to do with the day-to-day running of the company.

A.B. Pollock celebrated his 70th birthday at the company's 40th anniversary dinner.

A highlight was the inauguration of the Quarter Century Club. Employees who had worked for the company for 25 years or more went up to the podium to shake hands with A.B. and receive a gold watch, a gift for their wives, and six weeks paid holiday. In return, the employees presented A.B. with an illuminated scroll expressing their affection and loyalty.

Every employee received a new 1947 silver dollar which turned out to be part of a flawed batch from the Royal Mint. As a result, the dollars became valuable collectors items, which in 1996 were worth about $700. There were stories of enterprising Electrohome employees

The Horton-Electrohome washing machine, an example of the company's search for new products, was not a big seller, proving correct a prediction by A.B. Pollock.

machines and electric ironers under licence from the Horton Washing Machine Co. of the United States. At a directors meeting, A.B. Pollock voiced his opposition but was outvoted. The minutes record that A.B. said: "Although I oppose this program, I will work in all ways possible to make a success of this venture."

A.B.'s misgivings proved to be correct. The venture ran into problems when the Canadian government curtailed the volume of purchases made by Canadian companies in the U.S. The amount allowed was so small that the ceiling on Electrohome's purchases of parts from the Horton company was quickly reached and the company was unable to make washing machines or ironers for an entire year. To overcome the foreign exchange restrictions, the company decided to build its own tool and die setups and make the parts in Kitchener. As a result, Canadian-made washing machines bearing the Horton-Electrohome name were sold across Canada but sales never did reach a satisfactory level and after substantial losses, the company abandoned the washing machine field.

That was not the only new market to be explored. The appliance and metal products division, under the direction of Sebastian (Seb) Englert, developed a number of DC motors for use in car heaters, air conditioners and rear window defoggers, as well as a unique axle shifting mechanism for use on mid-sized truck differentials. These proved to be a very profitable item. At least 1,000 a week of the axle shifter motors were sold for over 30 years around the world. The division also added to its growing product line of three-inch diameter AC

making the rounds of local taverns trying to buy up the coins from unaware owners.

Continuing the tradition of searching for new business opportunities that would match its manufacturing capabilities, the company decided to make washing

of packaged hi-fi entertainment and gave Electrohome a head start over its competitors. The consoles were large pieces of furniture distinctively styled to match the interior of any home. The Princess was "a traditional period design embracing the classic 18th century Chippendale style," available in walnut with satinwood border or mottled striped and plain striped mahogany. The Tempora featured a handsome modern cabinet..."a triumph of cabinet artistry," also available in walnut or mahogany. All these new models were available with either the 6-tube, dual wave radio-phonograph combination or the 8-tube AM/FM chassis "for perfection in radio reception." The latter was described as the "Little Wonder" in some technical journals.

Product promotional material stated that both models were designed "so that the Webster 3-speed, fully automatic record changer and tuning panel is housed in the bureau-type drawer which leaves the top free for an expressive plant or flower arrangement. Ample record space is provided to conveniently accommodate 72 records in storage albums." The record changer—a first in Canada, the company proudly stated—came equipped with three spindles, one for each standard.

In an article in *Sparks and Chips*, under the heading of The Coming Trend!, Carl Pollock described FM radio receivers and the latest developments in recordings. Up until 1948, most Canadian manufacturers had been using pre-war technology for their products. According to C.A., "the only real aspect of postwar newness was achieved by creating quite different cabinet designs."

Two developments were to change the direction of

motors for oil burners, kitchen ventilators and other air moving appliances.

In the woodworking and furniture division, leather-topped tables and exquisite hand-painted cabinets were introduced under the Deilcraft name. The first postwar high performance phonograph, the Concorde, was offered in an elegant furniture-styled cabinet. It sold for $399. It was the forerunner of a move to combine the company's traditional skills in engineering, metalworking and woodworking to make a product which appealed to changing tastes. Three years later, responding to dealer suggestions, the company introduced Canada's first "hi-fi" radio-phono combination, a console containing amplifiers, tuners and speakers. It was the beginning the industry. One was the growing acceptance of FM band radio receivers with interference-free reception and better tone quality. The other was the introduction by Columbia Records of long-playing 33⅓ rpm recordings. Columbia's arch-rival, Victor, was caught off-guard but came out a year later with its "doughnut," a seven-inch disc that played at 45 rpm. Both new formats provided higher quality sound reproduction.

C.A. commented: "Both of these developments are distinct improvements...there is a greater realism, a greater sense of the actual presence of those who are doing the entertaining. All music lovers and listeners will want to take advantage of these truly new postwar achievements."

His article also made reference to developments in television..."a very desirable achievement which will play a tremendous part in the home entertainment business." He cautioned, however, that television was very technical and "so much more expensive a service to render to the public that it will grow more slowly than other services."

Selling TV receivers where signals are too weak for good reception can do much harm, he warned, because there is no poorer advertisement for any product or service than a disappointed disillusioned customer.

"Let us keep our feet on the ground and gain experience slowly so that when TV is established in Canada, we will be ready."

Television was an area which C.A. had been watching with keen interest. In a speech in November 1947, he had predicted that color TV sets would not be manufactured in Canada before 1955, even though U.S.

manufacturers had announced their intention of introducing color sets in the coming year.

At this time, there were no Canadian firms making even black-and-white television sets. The first major display of electronic television had been mounted at the Canadian National Exhibition in Toronto in 1939 and a year later, J.L. Baird patented a high definition color TV system in Britain. Development of the product was suspended during the war but resumed immediately afterwards at an energetic pace.

In the United States, it was common for people to watch television in department stores, bars, hotels, appliance stores, furniture stores and other public places. It was estimated that in 1945, one million

FM radio was incorporated in this radio-phonograph combination.

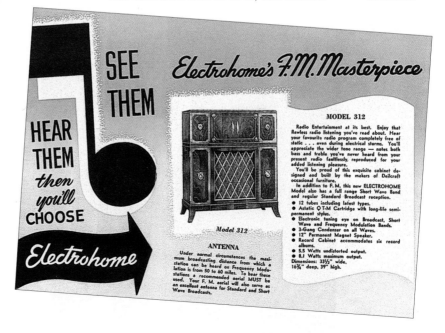

U.S. people had access to TV programming, yet only 6,000 sets had been sold.

In 1947, Canadian General Electric demonstrated a U.S.-manufactured TV set receiving a picture from the new station, WWDT in Detroit. The National Broadcasting Company (NBC) created the first network by linking four eastern stations. A year later, regular national network broadcasting began and the TV audience multiplied by 4,000 per cent as the number of cities served increased and the number of sets sold skyrocketed.

Carl Pollock had known for some time that television was going to play a major role in the company's future. In July 1948, the board of directors had agreed to spend $5,000 to buy 25

Television set assembly line, 1950.

The first Electrohome black-and-white television sets were made in 1949.

sets from Wells-Gardner in Chicago "for demonstration and testing in Plant 1 in Kitchener and in sales offices in Windsor and Niagara Falls." Howard Main, who was to become a long-serving senior executive, sold the first of these sets in Windsor. The path to the future was clear when Eatons ordered 50 TV sets.

The company was still struggling with cash-flow problems. The washing machine business was losing money and the government had imposed a heavy excise tax on the sales of radio sets.

Despite misgivings about the current cash shortage, the order prompted the board to allocate the funds to make the 50 sets from purchased parts. Key manufacturing personnel were sent to the Wells-Gardner plant in Chicago to learn the intricacies of TV manufacturing.

The result was the Electrohome Console TV, featuring a 12-inch screen, housed in "an exquisite period-design cabinet that will enhance any living room." Exhibited at the Canadian National Exhibition in August 1949, it was an instant success and in October 1949, a limited number of sets were made available to dealers.

The company announced that after extensive tests in all parts of Canada's TV area, the Electrohome TV had proven to excel, not only in the reproduction of clearer pictures but in audio tonal quality and cabinet design.

The fact was that at this early stage in the development of television, Canadian viewers had only one place to tune for programs—over the U.S. border. They joined their U.S. cousins watching Texaco Star Theatre with Milton Berle, which was so popular that it created a boom in TV set sales. Another performer, Ed Sullivan, took to the airwaves with a program called Toast of the Town, which was to last in one form or another for 23 years.

It wasn't long before a joke went around that it was easy to find your way around Canadian border cities without a compass because all the rooftop aerials pointed south. It was not until 1952 that Canadians could watch their own television programs originated by Canadian Broadcasting Corporation stations in Montreal and Toronto.

To ensure that buyers of Electrohome radios and TVs would receive good service from retailers carrying the company's products, a Toronto parts service depot was opened in 1949—the first of several to be opened in key cities across Canada.

Service included a personal call on the customer several days before the warranty expired to make any adjustments and to ensure complete customer satisfaction. In the days before cable television, the location of the receiving antenna was crucial in obtaining a good

picture. In certain areas, an adjustment of four inches could eliminate ghosting, interference and an unsatisfactory picture.

The company went to great lengths to cultivate dealer loyalty and to maintain a close dialogue with them on a number of topics, including advice on how to move inventory. One suggestion involved customers with older radios brought in for repair. Provide them with a new model while the old one is being repaired, the company suggested, and in no time the customer will be ordering a new one.

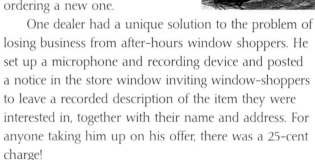

One dealer had a unique solution to the problem of losing business from after-hours window shoppers. He set up a microphone and recording device and posted a notice in the store window inviting window-shoppers to leave a recorded description of the item they were interested in, together with their name and address. For anyone taking him up on his offer, there was a 25-cent charge!

Canadians with black-and-white TV sets were not the only ones with rooftop aerials pointing south. In the United States, the superiority of FM radio had led to the introduction of FM broadcasting and Canadians with the correct antennas could pull in the signals of cross-border stations.

Customer service by Electrohome dealers was a major selling point.

Carl Pollock's long-time interest in owning a radio station prompted him to explore the idea of starting an FM station in Kitchener-Waterloo. If he wasn't to be allowed an AM station licence, perhaps he could convince the authorities to give him an FM licence. His market research included paying his son, John, then a high school student, to cycle around residential neighborhoods and count the number of recently-installed rooftop FM aerials. John couldn't remember the results of his "market research," but they obviously convinced Carl to proceed. His application for a licence was approved by the federal Department of Transport and CFCA-FM went on the air.

The station had a staff of about a dozen who planned an elaborate introductory program which included an 80-minute excerpt of the Pan Politae Club's 101 Minutes of Charm program, broadcast live from the K-W Collegiate auditorium. The major event of the evening, however, was a program called Hats Off to Our Neighbors, which, according to a report published in *Sparks and Chips*, honored "those people within our listening area who have done much to create the Canadian way of life through their outstanding work in the field of art, music, literature, medicine, public affairs and others."

Chris Fairly, one of several Electrohome employees who moved over to the station, was appointed commercial manager. She told the *Kitchener-Waterloo Record* that CFCA's policy was "to encourage local live talent in music, drama, etc. and we want to do as much as we can to develop this talent into a network calibre program."

The station went on to broadcast concerts by the Kitchener-Waterloo Symphony, of which C.A. Pollock was a founding director, as well as amateur contests and recitals by area pianists. For these, the radio station installed a Steinway grand piano in a studio built specially with rounded walls "for true reproduction."

Even though the radio station was owned by a separate company controlled by C.A., Electrohome joined in the effort to popularize the new medium by designing and manufacturing its own line of FM radio receivers. The static-free reception features of these sets were enthusiastically promoted by the company's salesmen and C.A. even arranged for FM radios to be installed on local streetcars running up and down King Street to give passengers a taste of higher quality sound.

A Steinway grand piano was installed at CFCA-FM Radio studio in downtown Kitchener.

Unfortunately, the people of Kitchener-Waterloo did not greet CFCA with the level of enthusiasm anticipated by Carl Pollock and his staff. Not enough local people could be convinced to tune into the new station and local businesses could not justify switching their advertising dollars from the AM station, CKCR, or from the local newspapers.

After a 28-month struggle, C.A. concluded that his timing was wrong. It was evident that the public was more interested in the new medium of television and he closed the station. It was his third disappointing foray into radio station ownership. His early interest in the medium had led him just before the war to apply to the governors of the Canadian Broadcasting Corporation for a local radio station licence. His application was denied but his enthusiasm remained and throughout the war he often thought of the day when he would own his own station. In 1947, he had applied for an AM licence was again turned down because it was felt that an additional station would hurt the economic position of the existing station in the Kitchener–Waterloo area.

The 1946 sale of shares in the company on the Toronto Stock Exchange had made it necessary to publish an annual report to shareholders, detailing the previous year's activities and indicating plans for the future. In its 1950 annual report, the company was able to report that "the first dividend in the history of operations was paid to shareholders on December 1, 1949." The dividend was 20 cents a share, based on net earnings of $81,912.09—almost double the profits of the previous year.

In his report to shareholders, A.B. Pollock stated that the improved profits reflected "improved external and internal operations and the standing of the company in the minds of its customers and the Canadian buying public." One of these internal improvements had been the introduction the year before of budgetary planning and controls for each department which A.B. said would result in major benefits for shareholders.

It was to be the founder's last annual report. The heart attack he had suffered earlier had taken its toll and he never really regained the vitality that had characterized his early years of building the company. On December 16, 1951, A.B. Pollock died at home at the age of 75.

Two years later, on Sept. 15, 1953, Mrs. Racie B. Pollock died at the family home on Benton Street where she and her husband had lived since the early days of the business.

C.A. Pollock took over as president of the company, a move his father had hoped and planned for in those earlier years when Carl's ambitions pulled him in other directions. He had been effectively in charge of the company for the past few years and his management style had brought respect from Electrohome employees at every level. He had recognized the significant changes facing the company as early as 1947, when he instigated the restructuring that created three manufacturing divisions.

The changes had been refined and improved upon as conditions continued to change in the early 1950s. C.A. presided over regular meetings of a management committee, which consisted of the managers of the three manufacturing divisions and the heads of the support services (accounting, purchasing, industrial relations). They combined their ideas and approaches to develop plans and policies for the future.

Several members of the committee were also members of the board of directors: C.A., as company president, was also chairman of the board; Gordon Tufts, senior vice-president and manager of the private brands division; Bill Curry, vice-president and head of Electrohome products; Clayton Allgeier, vice-president and works manager; Don Sykes, in charge of treasury and accounting, was secretary-treasurer of the company. Their presence on the board ensured a high level of communication from the operating side of the company to the shareholders.

The value of this type of communication was evident in 1952. The death of A.B. Pollock had not been the only bad news.

The postwar burst of enthusiastic consumer spending had tapered off. The Canadian government, blaming the effects of the Korean War, attempted to control inflation by increasing the manufacturing tax on home entertainment products to 35 per cent and imposed credit restrictions to discourage Canadians from going into debt.

These factors combined to produce what C.A. Pollock described as "a consumer goods business environment which was depressive in the extreme." Almost everything the company made was intended for the consumer. The radio, television, appliances and furniture businesses were crippled as orders dried up. The company lost more than $100,000—about the same as the previous year's profits.

In his report to shareholders, C.A. made a valiant attempt at optimism:

"The new (management) approach has modified many of the services and practices, making them appreciably less expensive and thereby reducing the break-even point. We expect, therefore, to operate profitably in the very competitive market of the near future."

The company introduced a new incentive and profit-sharing pension plan "which allows the employee to participate proportionally in the profits earned by the company so that not only is their retirement income assured, but each member of the organization has a sufficient incentive to make an even greater contribution to its operation."

As if the death of A.B. Pollock and the gloomy economic news were not enough, there was worse to come. On Friday, May 23, 1952, a worker in a spray booth at the Deilcraft furniture plant at Duke and Breithaupt Street, used a metal ferrous hammer instead of the copper-headed one provided for use in the vicinity of flammable materials. A spark ignited lacquer fumes and caused what the *Kitchener-Waterloo Record* was to describe as "the greatest local fire in years." The fire resulted in the death of Adolph Scharlach, a finisher, who had safely left the building only to return to retrieve a pair of shoes. Another employee, Peter Tarasiuk, was admitted to hospital with burns. Although a firewall stopped the flames from spreading, the fire ruined 12,000 square feet of the plant and caused hundreds of

"The greatest local fire in years" at Deilcraft furniture plant in 1952 resulted in one death. Firemen from several surrounding communities fought the blaze.

thousands of dollars in damage. In a statement the company paid tribute to the work of firemen from Kitchener, Waterloo and Preston who were called in to bring the fire under control. A TV set was donated to each fire station.

Furniture manufacturing was suspended until the finishing department was rebuilt, but production on the lower levels of the plant which sustained mainly water damage resumed within three weeks.

Despite all the setbacks, Carl Pollock's faith in the company's future remained unshaken. "We are expecting to go places in 1952-53," he told shareholders.

His optimism was well-founded. The earlier setbacks seemed to have been a watershed because immediately afterwards, the company's fortunes changed. Business grew by leaps and bounds. Production of radio and television sets could not keep up with demand. Deilcraft occasional furniture became an industry leader and electric motor and appliance sales achieved new levels.

The company changed its fiscal reporting year-end to Dec. 31 and in the next annual report, C.A. announced that sales for the previous eight months were higher than the entire year earlier. The 75% increase in sales resulted in a profit of $162,708 or $1.63 per share.

Looking ahead, C.A. forecast an even better year with sales increasing by 15-20 per cent. He said Electrohome products "are receiving an acceptance of the highest standing." This was partly the result of an expanded advertising budget of $50,000 to raise the public's awareness of the Electrohome brand name.

Although television had been nothing more than

Autumn leaf mahogany "Mardi Gras" radio-TV -phonograph combination was made in 1952. It was powered by 30 tubes in this pre-transistor era.

an experiment only four years earlier, the company's future success would be linked to the medium that was capturing the public's imagination. The annual report predicted that in 1953, "television will be the largest individual contributor to our sales volume. With the high level of public interest in this new medium of entertainment, education and communication, several prosperous years are in prospect."

In the spring of 1953, C.A. Pollock became a member of a business group which applied for a television station licence for Kitchener. His partners were Kitchener-Waterloo Broadcasting Company Ltd. (which operated CKCR Radio), and Famous Players Corporation, owners of a chain of movie theatres. The company they formed to apply for the licence for Channel 6 was called Central Ontario Television Ltd.

C.A. and Kitchener-Waterloo Broadcasting had previously applied for a licence and had been turned down. Famous Players had the same experience with an application for a licence for Toronto. At the time the Canadian Broadcasting Corporation was the sole arbiter of who would get TV station licences—and where. The only TV stations operating in Canada were operated by the CBC but pressure to establish privately-operated stations prompted the decision to grant licences in selected communities. Sudbury and London were the first two communities to get privately-owned stations and Kitchener-Waterloo soon followed.

Central Ontario Television found itself up against Grand Television Ltd., a company whose directors were Frowde Seagram of the well-known Waterloo distilling family, Senators Arthur C. Hardy and William D. Euler (another prominent Kitchener citizen), and H.A. Saunders, a Galt manufacturer.

Central Ontario Television won the battle and on Sept. 28, 1953, the company was granted a licence to operate Channel 13 in Kitchener. C.A. Pollock welcomed the news by saying that the station would emphasize local community service and would present "a fair number" of cultural programs.

The first signals from the new station—a test pattern—were broadcast on Christmas Eve, 1953, from a 205-foot tower on Baden Hill, the same property bought by C.A. for his ill-fated FM radio station.

On March 1, 1954, the *Kitchener-Waterloo Record* head-line announced: "TV Station Goes on Air Here Tonight." The fledgling company spent the first few months operating in temporary quarters on Young Street in downtown Kitchener, lent by John Wintermeyer, a prominent local lawyer who later became leader of the Ontario Liberal Party. A property at 864 King Street West, opposite Kitchener-Waterloo Hospital, was bought and converted to offices and studios. (The station is still in the same location).

In the months after being granted the licence, the pace of activity bordered on the frantic as staff were hired, equipment purchased and installed, and programming organized. *The Record* reported that the electronic equipment in the studio was worth $300,000.

Programs were to come from two sources: News and current affairs shows produced in the station's own studios, and programs on film obtained from the CBC or

CKCO-TV went on the air March 1, 1954.

other outside sources. A third source soon evolved—the delivery of CBC programs over a microwave network provided by CN-CP Communications.

The station's debut occurred toward the close of the hockey season and the CBC had announced its intention of broadcasting the final games of the Stanley Cup. The opportunity to provide as-it-happens coverage to capture new viewers was too good to pass up, except that the station had no facilities to connect with the CBC's new microwave relay station south of Galt (Cambridge).

A.G. (Sandy) Day, CKCO's chief engineer, looked out of his office window and saw a Public Utilities Commission water tower casting its shadow over the station property. His creative mind envisaged a dish antenna mounted on the water tower to receive a signal beamed from the microwave station. In a matter of weeks, the station was receiving a live CBC-TV signal from Toronto—just in time for the playoffs!

Many challenges were faced during the period leading up the March 1 opening. One involved an important piece of equipment, the kinescope projector, which fed the film image through a series of angled mirrors onto the ionoscope tube of the TV camera. One day when the staff were learning how to operate the equipment, smoke began to pour from the projector. Fortunately, the problem was located and repairs made in time for the station to start broadcasting on schedule.

Sandy Day was the only member of the station's management team to make the move from Electrohome, where he had been supervisor of TV and production engineer. The remaining members came from all over the world with one thing in common—they had experience in either radio, films or TV.

General manager was Eugene Fitzgibbons, who had worked for 20th Century Fox before joining Famous Players theatres. Operations manager was W.D. McGregor, who had radio experience with CFRB and CKFH in Toronto, and then was a TV instructor with the CBC. He later told how he'd written to Carl Pollock suggesting he'd like to run the new TV station.

"He wrote back and said he didn't think so. But I sneaked in the back door and I'm still here." Bill McGregor replaced Fitzgibbons when he returned to Famous Players and rose to become president of CKCO and a leading figure in the Canadian television industry.

W.D. (Bill) McGregor, CKCO operations manager, later became president.

Other members of the opening day staff were Peter Eakins, controller; Elena Gerngross, film editor, an Italian film actress who had worked at the CBC; her husband, Amedeo, former film cameraman who was the station's film librarian; Gerard Van Duyn, art director, from Holland; Don Hildebrand from Wingham, announcer; Robert Helm, video engineer, who had worked for the CBC; Bruce Lawson, telecine operator, who had worked for the National Film Board and CBC; Richard Weber of Kitchener, also a telecine operator with announcing experience at CKCR; and Kenneth Horne, maintenance engineer, with wide experience in film and TV in England.

The opening night program, produced by Famous Players, was hosted by Win Barron, the voice of Paramount News. The film of the formal affair shows the mayors of Kitchener, Waterloo, Preston, Galt and Brantford—obviously uncomfortable in front of the camera—performing an on-air ribbon-cutting ceremony with Carl Pollock, who was just as obviously relaxed and at ease.

C.A. praised the staff for getting the station on the air two months ahead of schedule and promised "a complete program of information and entertainment including color, when it becomes available."

The opening of CKCO-TV added to C.A.'s already busy schedule. In addition to his Electrohome commitments, he was a frequent speaker on behalf of the Chamber of Commerce and other business-related organizations.

He was passionately committed to ensuring that his companies would keep abreast of developments in management practices and make employees aware of the benefits of continued education and self-improvement. The decentralized management structure he had put in place was constantly being refined and improved. He said: "It will be through the best business methods that companies will grown and expand."

As 1954 drew to a close, Carl Pollock could look back with satisfaction at the accomplishments of the companies that were his life. Electrohome was poised to capitalize on the unique combination of capabilities in the home entertainment and furniture fields by increasing its product lines and expanding its share of

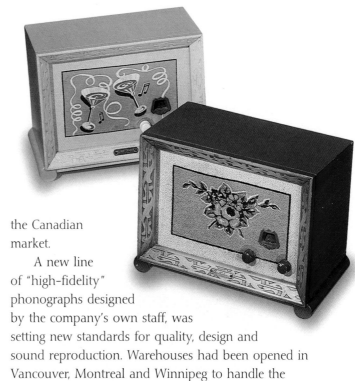

Examples of "picture radios" made in the mid-1950s.

the Canadian market.

A new line of "high-fidelity" phonographs designed by the company's own staff, was setting new standards for quality, design and sound reproduction. Warehouses had been opened in Vancouver, Montreal and Winnipeg to handle the increased business.

The Deilcraft product line, which up to this point had been confined to occasional tables, was expanded by the addition of dinette suites. This product line was offered in traditional and contemporary styles and met with instant success.

The defence and industrial contracts group had made its first profit and was expected to increase its business in 1955. The division had been created as a separate operating unit a year earlier to take advantage of a Canadian government program designed to foster "home-grown" manufacturing competence.

The motor and metal products division had survived a year of lower revenues due to a decline in sales of small motors to automobile manufacturers. The division made a concerted effort to replace the business and found customers for new products such as electric can openers and blower wheels. New export business was found in the United States, Holland and Denmark, a move which duplicated the sale of spring-wound motors to China and Australia in the 1920s and helped set the direction the company was to take.

Exquisitely hand-painted (Chinoiserie) wooden cabinets were featured on some TV sets.

The big news concerned the company's TV set business. Despite a bout of price-cutting in the TV and appliance retail market, sales were the highest in the company's history and Electrohome was making a profit.

Electrohome engineers had designed a new 22-tube deluxe chassis which could pull in programs from U.S. stations south of the border, unlike some less-expensive competitive sets on the market. To accommodate the new models, TV production facilities had been redesigned and manufacturing capabilities doubled.

In his report to shareholders, C.A.'s optimism was evident.

"Electrohome is well equipped, compared with many of its home entertainment and home furnishing competitors, in that its field of business experience includes the electronic, electrical, woodworking and metal working industries.

"Under the impetus of research, all of these fields are expanding faster than at any previous time in Canadian business history.

"Electrohome is a Canadian company throughout. During these years of rapid growth of Canada's population and economy, the board of directors and the divisional managers are working to develop business characteristics and facilities which, in their estimation, should earn for the company a continued place in Canada's future."

1954 brochure extolls virtues of Electrohome's "furniture-styled" radio-phonographs.

Electrohome Furniture Styled **RADIOS** with CABINETS by Deilcraft

Arthur Bell Pollock, founder of Electrohome, 1877-1951.

A.B. Pollock:
An eye for life's finer things

When he died in 1951 at the age of 75, Arthur Bell Pollock left his home on Benton Street and his Muskoka cottage filled with fine silver, oriental rugs, antique furniture and valuable artwork. They reflected a man who loved the finer things in life, according to his grandson, John A. Pollock, now chairman and chief executive officer of the company.

Despite humble beginnings, he was exposed at an early age to the privileged lives of Sir Thomas Lipton and some of the wealthiest men in the United States who were members of the New York Yacht Club. His Metropolitan Opera singer friends Harry Boehmer and Edward Johnston also opened doors to a world patronized by the well-to-do and influential. When he resigned as secretary of the Yacht Club to return home to Berlin, the club members presented him with a gold ring containing two large diamonds, as a measure of their esteem.

The New York experience must have been an exciting existence for a young man from rural Ontario. It obviously formed tastes and stimulated interests which never left him. His boyhood exposure to music influenced his choice of business career and led to the founding of the company. It was an interest which was ever-present, according to John Pollock.

"The Benton Street house had a music room where Grandmother (Racie Boehmer Pollock, herself an accomplished singer), would entertain us.

"In 1918, he bought a Muskoka cottage, on a small island in Lake Rosseau, from the Massey family. We would go there every summer. At first, 'Pater' as his grandchildren called A.B., would take the train from Kitchener on Friday nights to Toronto, another train to Gravenhurst and then a steamer up the lake to the cottage, arriving on Saturday morning. Later, when automotive travel became more popular, he would

Arthur Pollock at his Muskoka cottage.

A.B. (right) with grand-daughter Barbara, entertaining business collegues in Chicago, 1946.

on a business trip to Chicago when she was in her early teens.

"We went on the train and he knew everybody. We stayed at the Drake Hotel and he even took me with him to meet his friends at a nightclub. For a 13-year-old girl from Kitchener, that was quite an experience."

He regarded himself as more of an expert in business and finance and was content to leave the engineering and production problems to his partner, Alex Welker.

At work, he was a warm and friendly person, encouraging employees to get involved with sports and other social activities. It was obvious from the stories told by many employees that A.B. was a strong believer that team spirit on the sports field would extend to the workplace. He was disappointed and hurt when his employees formed a union, which he saw as coming between management and members of the company. Nevertheless, he accepted this change as a sign of the times and learned from the experience.

He knew everyone by name. "He never came into the office without speaking to each person," recalled long-time employee Gordon Fowler.

Agnes Ellert, who started in 1931 and worked for the company for 46 years, mainly in customs, export and purchasing, told how A.B. was responsible for starting a popular office practice:

"He asked me what he should do to observe his birthday. I jokingly suggested buying everyone a box of chocolates. On the day, he came in with a box of chocolates for everyone in the plant and office. It became a tradition that when someone had a birthday, they

drive up, even though most of the roads were gravel until the 1950s."

The cottage is still in the family's possession, although the Benton Street home was sold and later demolished.

Since he never had a daughter, A.B. doted on C.A.'s wife, Helen, and later his grand-daughter, now Mrs. Barbara Steele. John Pollock recalls his mother being taken by A.B. on shopping sprees to New York.

As president and the company's first salesman, A.B. travelled extensively across Canada and to bigger U.S. cities such as Chicago and New York, building up a large network of friends and business contacts which over the years led to several advantageous moves. Barbara Steele tells of being taken by her grandfather

A.B. with Carl's children, John and Barbara, circa 1950.

provided their immediate staff with a box of chocolates."

In her 50th anniversary history of Electrohome, author Edna Staebler wrote:

"His friendliness, innate honesty and belief in the value of work were impressed for all time on the character of the industry to which he had devoted his life. His death was deeply regretted by the many friends he had worked with. A Czech immigrant spoke with tears in his eyes of the help A.B. had given him when he came to Canada, afraid and alone. His supervisors talked of the happy times when he'd taken them to his island cottage in Muskoka and urged them to eat more fried pork sausage and mashed potatoes. His secretary ruefully recalled the busy day when he had dictated one hundred letters."

His personality and integrity were summed up in a tribute to the founder contained in the 40th anniversary edition of *Sparks and Chips* in 1947:

"Mr. Pollock has not only made a success of his business, he has also made a success of his life. He counts his friends by the hundreds and his genial personality and hospitality are known from coast to coast. It has been said that a gauge of a man's success is the respect and esteem which his fellow men have for him. This being true, Mr. Pollock is surely an outstanding success. We are proud of our president, we have confidence in his leadership, and we know him as our friend."

CHAPTER SIX

1955-1969 The Golden Years

Circa 75 home entertainment package, introduced in 1967, embodied futuristic design concepts. The circular console was described as "a communications centre in your own home."

"The latter half of the twentieth century will be Canada's own if we Canadians make it so!"

These were the words often used by Carl Pollock to inspire business, labor and community leaders in speeches he made across Canada in the late 1950s. They represented an attitude and approach that was to propel Electrohome through one of the most successful periods in the company's history—some called them the Golden Years.

The 1,050 members of the Electrohome family celebrating the company's 50th anniversary in 1957 would have found it hard to imagine the Electrohome which was to develop over the next 20 years–propelled by Carl Pollock's drive to "make it so."

Seated at long rows of tables in the Kitchener Auditorium, they spent a nostalgic evening looking back, reminiscing and happily greeting former colleagues now retired. Even Alex Welker was there, welcomed back to the organization he had spent many years helping to build. His contribution was recognized by the gift of a high fidelity phonograph and a life membership in the Quarter Century Club. While C.A. Pollock was happy to look backwards that night, he couldn't resist the opportunity to point the way forward: "Our 50th anniversary is also the beginning of another half century of business and it is a time to look ahead."

C.A. said the company was better known than at any other time in its history because of customer-oriented

W. E. CURRY
Electrohome Products

J. G. TUFTS
Private Trade Label

C. A. POLLOCK
President

C. ALLGEIER
Deilcraft

S. P. ENGLERT
Motor and Metal
Products

W. N. HEMPHILL
Purchasing
and Customs

N. J. LONG
Industrial
and
Public Relations

D. S. SYKES
Finance and
Accounting

GEORGE EITEL
Design

F. A. O. BANKS
Technical Products

1907 Electrohome 50 1957

The executive team in 1957, the company's 50th anniversary year.

sales policies, unique products and trend-setting public and industrial relations programs. But the achievements which made him so proud in 1957 would pale by comparison with what lay ahead.

Under his dynamic leadership, Electrohome would become a household name in home entertainment, furniture and numerous other consumer products—across Canada and in many other countries.

A never-ending search for new markets would bring in business from far and wide. Sub-fractional electric motors, originally developed in the 1930s to provide the power for phonographs, would be found in an array of nationally-branded automotive, consumer and industrial products.

By the end of the Sixties, sales figures would triple to $44.5 million, and there would be over 2,250 people working in 1.2 million square feet of manufacturing space and five Canadian branch offices.

Among a list of new products would be electronic organs, educational television sets and monitors, the first varactor-tuned television, multi-channel stereo and cassette tape players. With the company's focus on advanced engineering and aesthetic designs, new ideas and new products would become the hallmark of Electrohome.

These peaks of achievement would not come without some disappointments and changes in direction. As the Fabulous Fifties came to a close, C.A. would see both challenge and opportunities ahead.

The postwar "population explosion" had brought a boom in new housing construction which in turn triggered a demand for consumer products on a scale never before experienced. North Americans had changed their living habits as they adapted to television.

Television's effect on everyday life was described in the catalogue of a 1995 exhibition mounted in Toronto by the Royal Ontario Museum and MZTV Museum, Toronto.

"Movie attendance dropped, drive-in theatres closed, *Life* and the other picture magazines folded, *TV Guide* became a publishing sensation.

"The middle class American woman needed persuading that a large box approximately the size of a washing machine, containing an exotic-sounding technology

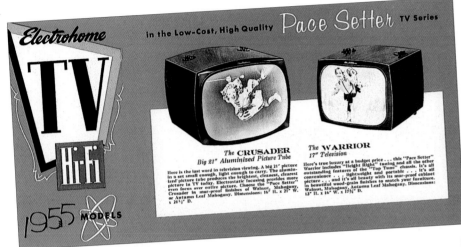

In the Low-Cost, High Quality *Pace Setter* TV Series

The **CRUSADER**
Big 21" Aluminized Picture Tube

Here is the last word in television viewing. A big 21" picture in a set small enough to carry. The aluminized picture tube produces the brightest, cleanest, clearest picture in TV today. Electrostatic focusing provides more even focus over entire picture. Choose the "Pace Setter" Crusader in mar-proof finishes of Walnut, Mahogany, or Autumn Leaf Mahogany. Dimensions: 16" H. x 21" W. x 21½" D.

The **WARRIOR**
17" Television

Here's true luxury at a budget price . . . this "Pace Setter" Warrior includes "Height Right" tuning and all the other outstanding features of the "Top Tune" chassis. It's all convenience . . . lightweight and portable . . . It's all picture . . . and it's all beauty with its mar-proof cabinet in beautiful wood-grain finishes to match your furniture, in beautiful Walnut, Mahogany, Autumn Leaf Mahogany. Dimensions: 13" H. x 16" W. x 17¾" D.

called the cathode ray tube, was neither intrusive nor invasive in her most respectable living space, that on the contrary it was enhancing of that space and ought to be accorded a permanent position as a focal object.

"Marketing television for the postwar home meant designing elegant furniture with dignified names...and adorning them in magazine layouts with flowers, books and family portraits. Magazines of the day instructed the homemaker on how to place the television and how to arrange the furniture around it for a clear view."

Carl Pollock was determined that Electrohome, with its unique electronic and furniture-making capabilities, would take advantage of the unfolding market opportunities. .

By the time of the 50th anniversary dinner, a sparkling new electronic manufacturing plant had been built on Wellington Street North in Kitchener. The $650,000 building was officially opened during the 1957 annual shareholders meeting. The 103,000 square foot combination office and factory provided the ultimate in production

efficiencies for manufacturing television, radio, high fidelity phonographs and other electronic equipment.

A slogan, still displayed over the door, was a reflection of an approach that had been a constant theme since the company's earliest days. It says: "Through these doors pass quality minded people." A.B. Pollock always insisted that "quality is the best salesman a company can have." From the beginning, he wanted products that were technically excellent and "possess an appearance suitable for the living rooms which they would grace."

A year later, in the 1958 annual report, C.A. reported that the cost efficiencies resulting from the new plant had contributed to record after-tax profits of almost half a million dollars, an increase of over 72 per cent over the previous year. Investors echoed C.A.'s optimism by over-subscribing a $1 million debenture issue to provide more working capital.

In 1959, the 950 employees who belonged to the profit-sharing retirement plan celebrated a major mile-

C.A. Pollock hosted government and business leaders at 1957 opening of Wellington Street plant.

stone: Contributions passed the $1 million mark. In the eight years since the plan was started in 1952, the company's sales had doubled. Members contributed 5% of their earnings and the company added 25% of annual profit before taxes after deducting enough money to provide a 5% return on capital investment. Plan members received a share of the profit sharing allocation based on years of service and their earnings.

C.A. was ahead of his time in his attitude toward the people who worked for the company. Policies that were commonplace at Electrohome in the 1950s and 1960s would be announced with great fanfare elsewhere as radically new thinking 30 years later.

He would always refer to employees as "members." He said that at the foundation of a healthy and growing business "are interested, able and well-trained people."

C.A. introduced numerous policies to ensure good employee relations. He always referred to them as "members."

"These qualifications of an Electrohome member employee are stimulated by a company objective which asks management to provide a working environment in which all members may obtain the vital satisfaction achievable through a job well done. Factors which contribute to good morale and team spirit are working conditions, health and safety, operating responsibilities and advancement opportunities, remuneration, welfare benefits and labor relations as well as opportunities for incentive earnings and profit sharing."

C.A.'s attitude toward employees was reflected in the quality of relations with the union. In 1960, the company signed its first three-year contract with Local 30, Amalgamated Workers Union. Under the agreement, the work week was reduced from 45 to 40 hours without loss of take-home pay.

He was also a tireless promoter of products made in Canada. He wrote:

"We continue to draw to the attention of Canadians the benefits to be realized through the expansion of research, engineering, design and manufacturing in our land so abounding in natural resources."

In 1959, just before the company shut down for its annual summer vacation, each employee was given a Buy Canadian bumper sticker. He also said: "If Canadians wish to remain an independent country, our citizens and our business people must be motivated to retain our birthright, which is the opportunity to do the developing and operating of much of our Canadian society and economy."

The expansion which characterized the late 1950s was not confined to the electronic products area. Buoyed by the successes of the past few years, C.A. led his team into a series of new ventures as he sought to capitalize on the opportunities that were unfolding. It seemed as if his restless energy would never stop finding new products and new markets to explore.

The Deilcraft furniture division had built up a

KEEP CANADIANS WORKING

Bumper stickers with this slogan were distributed to all employees in 1959.

Hand-finishing operation illustrates how Deilcraft furniture earned a high quality reputation. Ten percent of all wooden living room furniture sold in Canada bore the Deilcraft name.

respectable 10 per cent share of all wooden living room furniture in Canada. Upholstered furniture and bedroom suites had been added to the product line. As Canadians began asking for high quality, custom-made furniture, the opportunity to capitalize on the Deilcraft name led to another area of expansion.

Carl Pollock and his wife Helen had seen high fashion decorators' showrooms in Chicago and New York and asked themselves: "Why not in Toronto?" Their first showroom, at 50 York Street in downtown Toronto, was designed by Helen Pollock and her daughter, Barbara. The official opening was attended by 60 interior decorators and designers, as well as members of the news media.

It was decided to group the manufacturing and sale of these high quality furniture lines under the newly-formed Albon Reproductions Division. The name, suggested by Helen Pollock, was the surname of an aunt from St. Catharines who was one of the few female interior decorators in Ontario in the early 1900s. It was

also the given name of Helen's brother, John Albon, who was one of the first casualties of mustard gas while serving with the British Expeditionary Force in France during the First World War.

Albon Reproductions went on to develop a partnership in Canada with Knoll Associates of New York, a company that had made a name for its avant-garde approach to interior design. Under the arrangement, Deilcraft manufactured Knoll-designed furniture including large volume runs of chrome-trimmed desks. Knoll provided the sales and marketing expertise and were successful in obtaining an order for furnishings for Toronto's award-winning city hall. The firm of Lief Jacobsen was contracted to make some of the Knoll metal furniture pieces, although most were made in Kitchener. Albon also sold high quality wooden and wrought iron furniture made by several U.S. manufacturers such as Woodard and Charak. A second showroom on Eglinton Avenue was opened to display these products.

Example of high quality furniture sold under Albon Reproductions name.

The Technical Products Department was an early example of how the company explored new product opportunities. The department, an outgrowth of the Defence and Industrial Contracts Division formed in 1952, was the exclusive distributor in Canada for two British companies and another based in Massachusetts. The products they sold included industrial radio frequency induction heating equipment, plastic welding equipment, as well as electrical and electronic measuring devices, mechanical and electrical counters, elevator braking systems and related controls. All were an indication of the increasing importance of advanced technology to the company's future strength.

In addition, the company was involved in a short-lived joint venture with the giant Raytheon Corporation of Waltham, Mass., which had won a Canadian government contract to design and build a new airport radar surveillance system as part of the country's air traffic control system. The contract stipulated that the equipment had to be manufactured in Canada.

As a result of previous contacts relating to TV manufacturing, Carl Pollock persuaded Raytheon to establish a radar manufacturing plant in Waterloo. He had several motives, chief among them a desire to attract a pool of engineering expertise to the Kitchener-Waterloo area which would be available to Electrohome, instead of having to compete with the attractions of Toronto and Montreal. The same motivation triggered his involvement in the creation of the University of Waterloo during the same period.

A new company, Raytheon Canada Ltd., was created early in 1956 with Carl Pollock as president and Electrohome's Donald Sykes as secretary and assistant treasurer. Raytheon provided the general manager, Ross Cann, and a treasurer and assistant secretary. Electrohome invested $50,000 for a 25 per cent share. The company began operations on Bridgeport Road in Waterloo and later built a much larger research and manufacturing facility on Phillip Street, also in Waterloo. Electrohome's association with Raytheon Canada was discontinued in April 1958, by which time its investment had doubled. Faced with having to invest considerably more, Electrohome's directors opted to accept Raytheon's offer to buy the 25 per cent share for the amount of its investment, $100,000.

By 1960, company sales had risen to $15.1 million, reflecting steady growth over the previous five years, although television sales had not reached their anticipated levels and there was a worrying decline of car and home radio sales due to competition from Japanese transistorized sets. (The transistor had been invented in 1947 by American

High fidelity radio for "hi-fi sound."

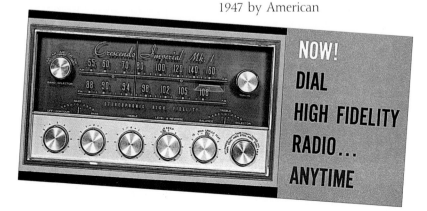

NOW! DIAL HIGH FIDELITY RADIO... ANYTIME

William Shockley but it was the Japanese who pioneered their use in solid state consumer electronic devices. It was a trend that was to become all too familiar to North American manufacturers).

One new product which was expected to do well was the stereo phonograph. Confusion among retailers and consumers regarding the difference between stereophonic and high fidelity sound was clarified by Carl Pollock:

"High fidelity means the quality and musical realism of the reproduction whereas stereophonic denotes a sense of the physical location of the source of the music.

"If the drums are on one side of the orchestra and the singer on the opposite side, the stereo listener receives these location impressions from the music reproduced in his home."

The Sixties was to become a watershed in history. The first of the postwar babies had reached their teens and were being brought up in front of the television set. One cultural historian credited—or blamed—television for "inadvertently levelling traditional social distances, resulting in challenges to hierarchies based on age, gender and political office."

The Sixties brought flower children, psychedelic clothing and the miniskirt. Canadians began to shed their cautious conservative image and students and young people, following the lead set by their counterparts in the United States and Britain, questioned and sometimes rejected many established social norms and values.

It was an era in which television would create a shared culture. Canadians joined viewers around the world watching Bonanza and Disneyland each week, as well as such home-grown shows as Hockey Night in Canada, Front Page Challenge and The Juliette Show.

Television provided all of us with a ringside seat to world events—the TV debates between John F. Kennedy and Richard Nixon, the drama of the Cuban Missile Crisis, the Beatles on the Ed Sullivan Show and the first man in space, Yuri Alexeyvich Gagarin, a Russian, on April 12, 1961. In the home entertainment industry, there were shocking revelations of rigged quiz games and payola in the phonograph record industry.

But the pivotal event that changed the way we regarded television was the assassination of John F. Kennedy in Dallas and the subsequent murder—live on TV—of Lee Harvey Oswald by Jack Ruby, on November 23, 1963. Newsweek magazine described the social significance of this mind-numbing sequence of events like this:

"Almost from the moment the horror occurred, television changed. It was no longer a small box containing entertainment, news and sports; suddenly, it was a window opening onto violently unpredictable life in Washington and Dallas."

The magazine's analysis was to become even more significant later in the Sixties as television brought the tragedies and terrors of the war in Vietnam into living rooms on a daily basis.

Toronto historian Marshall McLuhan postulated that "the medium is the message," arguing that television was "a totally new technology which demands different sensory responses." It was not, as its critics insisted, "merely a degraded form of print technology."

The Sixties brought a huge build-up of demand for consumer goods, which reached a crescendo in 1965 when the first color television sets became widely available. The ever-increasing demand in North America had not gone unnoticed by Far East manufacturers, who flooded the market with low-cost black and white television sets, radios and hi-fi phonographs. Like every other North American manufacturer, Electrohome experienced declining sales of these products.

Thanks to the company's diversified base, however, the blow to consumer electronics was softened by successes in home furnishings, electrical appliances and electric motors.

For the Deilcraft division particularly, the Sixties were a time of triumph. A team of talented designers led by George Eitel and including John Murray and Luigi Tiengo won numerous awards for their innovative approaches.

They were extremely successful with a new marketing concept based on the "correlation" of home furnishings with entertainment products. Deilcraft bedroom suites, dinette suites, occasional tables, lamps, chesterfields, chairs and Electrohome hi-fi and television sets were grouped into design "families" bearing such names as Florentine and Monterrey.

"No other company in Canada or the United States can offer such a correlation to the modern housewife who cares about her home and its interior decoration," proclaimed company literature.

Carl Pollock's deep commitment to the excellence of Canadian design was reflected in his 1962 appointment to the newly-formed 17-member National Design Council created the by federal government to improve Canadian product design and packaging. Following the death of George Eitel in 1961, C.A. brought in Gordon L. Duern, a talented designer, as manager of a newly-created product styling division. Eitel was not the only long-time contributor to the company's success whose talents were lost. James Gordon Tufts, who joined the company in 1929 and had served as senior vice-president for 10 years, working primarily on sales of private brand products, also died in 1961.

The success in the home furnishings area found the company scrambling at times to keep up with the demand. Despite the installation of a $250,000, half-mile-long finishing line at the Deilcraft plant at Duke and Breithaupt Streets, an additional 45,000 square feet was leased in the former Lang Tanning building in downtown Kitchener to make bedroom furniture. Another building at Duke and

Shanley Streets, used mainly to store bedroom and dinette suites, was enlarged.

It seemed as if every month there was an announcement of another new product, a new market, more employees and more production facilities.

The original metal products business was the foundation for a new Appliance, Lighting and Heating Division. Headed by Donald F. MacRae, its mandate was to design and sell fans, forced air and baseboard heaters, air conditioners and humidifiers and air purifiers, as well as an expanding line of electrical fixtures.

The company bought Campbell Electric Ltd., a Brantford lighting manufacturer with 35 employees.

Campbell's general manager, Homer Stickney, headed the operation. He later became sales manager of the appliance division under Ron Johnson. Manufacture of the metal components of the firm's 150 different lamp designs was transferred to Electrohome's Victoria Street plant and ultimately led to the development of a new "metal spinning" technique used for both lamps and a futuristic bubble stereo design. The addition of the lighting line resulted in Deilcraft lamps, many of them the work of a talented young designer, Michael Baldwin, being sold to Canadian embassies around the world, as well as military bases, hotels, hospitals, steamships and railway cars. They were also incorporated into Deilcraft contract furnishings supplied to college residences at the University of Waterloo.

Another Sixties home entertainment success was

Campell Electric of Brantford, acquired by Electrohome, added 150 lamp designs to the home furnishings product line.

the first home electronic organ to be made in Canada, a product which went on to enjoy many years of successful sales.

Despite the competition from the Far East, sales continued to climb and the company's designers and engineers were kept busy developing newer and better products, driven by C.A.'s consuming dedication to the idea that Canadians could design and manufacture products as good as any in the world.

The pace of business and new approaches to the way products were merchandised prompted another reorganization of the company's management structure in the early Sixties. Marketing requirements became the engine driving product operations, with finance and administrative services being the only centralized functions.

The executive committee headed by C.A provided overall direction. Other members were Donald S. Sykes, executive vice-president, finance; Clayton Allgeier, vice-president, industrial relations; and Howard W. Main, vice-president, marketing and sales.

In 1963, the division managers were Norman E. Bartlett, private trade label; Gordon L. Duern, product styling; Seb P. Englert, motor and metal products; Leo F. Fitzpatrick, consumer products merchandising; David H. Johnston, consumer products engineering and manufacturing: Jim King, Deilcraft; Harold J. Ruetz, consumer products contracts; and Maurice G. Monteith, industrial relations.

To bring sales, marketing, finance and other office operations under one roof, 42,000 square feet was added to the Wellington Street building in 1963 at a cost of

$500,000. By then, even the manufacturing facilities at Wellington Street were overcrowded and the company leased 14,000 sq. ft. of the former Marsland Precision Engineering plant on Regina St. in Waterloo. It was the company's ninth manufacturing plant in Kitchener-Waterloo.

About 40 people were moved there to assemble mantel radios, intercoms, portable phonos, speakers, tape recorders, and car radios. One new product made there was a "satellite" speaker system which dispersed stereo sound beyond the cabinet. This was introduced at a trade show in Chicago at a time when the launch of the Russian Sputnik space satellite was in the news. A U.S. Customs official read the product description, "two satellites," on the customs manifest and became suspicious that Electrohome was smuggling Russian satellites into the United States. He immediately ordered the truck to be unloaded so that he could see for himself that the satellites were indeed stereo speakers.

of Canadians for buying products from the United States. It was a continuing theme in the speeches he gave across the country. But he didn't blame the Americans.

"For all their genius for salesmanship, the Americans cannot sell us a product we do not buy or loan us a dime we do not borrow."

C.A. was very aware that Electrohome had been just as guilty in its buying practices. Back in the late Fifties,

the company was importing 70 per cent of the parts required for its stereo and hi-fi sets. C.A. was determined to reverse the flow. He encouraged the use of Canadian suppliers and there were numerous local companies which flourished as a result of supplying Electrohome with components. By the end of 1962, only seven per cent of components were imported and the company was exporting more than it imported.

C.A. also set a goal of exporting at least 25 per cent of Electrohome production by 1967, Canada's centennial year. David Lowater, who had started with the company in electronics engineering, was named export sales manager. His marketplace was anywhere in the world except the United States and Canada. One target was Canadian government offices around the world—an ideal setting to promote Electrohome products to overseas buyers. As a result of intensive efforts, Electrohome stereos, television sets and Deilcraft furniture became standard items in Canada's many overseas government facilities.

By 1965, Carl Pollock reported that Electrohome products were being sold in 23 countries. Sales of subfractional horsepower motors reached the five million mark with orders from such countries as New Zealand, Sweden and West Germany.

This successful drive to increase export sales was being matched in the United States. A new company was incorporated, International Electrohome Inc., with Howard Main as president. An extensive marketing

campaign opened up more than 500 U.S. dealer outlets and sales increased dramatically.

American consumers apparently loved the futuristic styling of Electrohome stereo hi-fi and TV sets, particularly bubble top phonographs and pedestal configurations. The design idea, using spun aluminum, came from Keith McQuarrie of the metal products division.

Some U.S. retailers set up Canadian Rooms in their stores devoted solely to the company's products. In a short time, the office and warehouse in a Chicago suburb were too small and larger premises were found.

The company's export program was recognized in 1964 when C.A. was presented with Ontario's highest industrial award for achievements in exporting and import replacements.

Increased business in the United States was also matched on the domestic front. Carl Pollock called 1962 "the most significant in our 55-year history." Sales increased by almost 30 per cent to $21.1 million and profits were $512,925, up by 29 per cent.

Sales of the Electrohome-Kinsman electronic organ reached new heights as did Deilcraft furniture. Carl Pollock attributed the growing acceptance of Electrohome consumer products in both Canada and the United States to the "forward look of our styling." The correlation concept was a huge success and justified the $500,000 a year the company was investing in design and engineering research.

Another significant reason was the way in which the company treated its customers. A survey of retailers resulted in 74% of dealers naming Electrohome as "the one company which operates an ideal policy. No volume discounts...no special deals. They choose their dealers on the basis of reputation, activity and financial responsibility. They supply consistently good products at fair competitive prices."

In 1963, the Deilcraft division raised its sights by joining forces with Sunshine Office Equipment Ltd. of Waterloo to make a line of prestige wooden office furniture, another market which offered opportunities for growth.

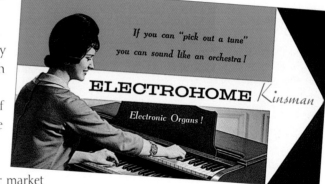

If you can "pick out a tune" you can sound like an orchestra!

ELECTROHOME *Kinsman*

Electronic Organs!

The first home electronic organ to be made in Canada enjoyed many years of successful sales.

Production facilities at the Duke Street plant were still strained, despite the relocation of some production facilities to the Lang building. It was obvious that the old plant was not the place for high volume furniture manufacturing and a search began for new premises.

It was a timely move inasmuch as the Kitchener-Waterloo economy was reflecting the booming Sixties economy.

The 1961 population of Kitchener had been close to 75,000 but predictions of growth prompted a group of leading businessmen to mastermind the development of a 500-acre industrial park in the southwest corner of the city. The objective was to encourage local companies

to expand and to attract new business to the growing community. Their timing was impeccable. In the next 10 years, while the population grew to 112,000, there was remarkable growth in manufacturing and employment: From 196 manufacturers to 509...15,200 employees to 32,000...$232 million of goods produced to over one billion dollars.

Electrohome was one of the early purchasers of land in the new industrial park. A 60-acre site across from the huge new B.F. Goodrich Canada tire manufacturing plant was bought in 1963. A $500,000 warehouse was built first, followed by a $3.5 million, 400,000 square foot plant for the manufacture of cabinetry and furniture. It was the largest single plant in Canada devoted to the manufacture of such products—a far cry from the original Elmira plant with its 30,000 square feet and 50 employees making phonograph cabinets. The 400 Deilcraft employees were moved from the factory at Duke and Breithaupt Streets. A veteran of the division, Gerry McDonnell, was promoted from woodworking produc-

tion manager to manufacturing manager of the new plant. Described as a man "who lived and breathed sawdust," McDonnell started as a production worker in 1940. His increasing managerial responsibilities had matched the growth of the Deilcraft division and he was credited with making the Deilcraft name synonymous with quality.

The need for trained employees to fill 200 new jobs at the new plant was a concern. Citing a severe shortage of Canadian workers, company officials said they would have to import skilled woodworkers from Europe and conduct training programs so that current employees could upgrade their skills.

In 1966, Electrohome bought a controlling interest in Hawkesville Lumber Ltd., which included a sawmill and timber stands of oak, elm and cherry. The intent was to reduce lumber inventories, improve raw material costs and ensure better quality.

At the opening of the new woodworking plant, C.A. proudly listed the company's accomplishments in the remarkable 10-year period since the 50th anniversary in 1957:

"The only company in Canada with the self-sufficiency to research and completely engineer and design its radio, hi-fi, television and electronic organ products.

"Canada's largest and best-equipped engineering and design facilities and personnel devoted to creating home entertainment products.

"Completely engineered and designed the only Canadian color television receiver—accepted as outstanding in performance in both Canada and the United States.

"Designed the only Canadian black and white portable television set with transistors instead of tubes and capable of being operated on direct current or batteries.

"Largest Canadian producer of sub-fractional horse-power electric motors with annual production of well over a million units."

After listing these accomplishments, C.A. paraphrased an old anecdote by predicting: "You ain't see nothin' yet!"

He was right—and color television made it happen.

As late as 1965, color TV transmission by Canadian stations had not been approved by the government, even though a large percentage of the population could watch programs in color from stations just across the U.S. border.

The Envoy, a portable black and white TV set was the first in Canada to be made with transistors instead of tubes. It could be plugged into a car's cigarette lighter.

Electrohome had sold a few color sets but the market needed the impetus that would come with color programming originating in Canada.

C.A. was critical of the government's tardiness. "Unless color broadcasting is allowed immediately, new and larger antennas will appear on rooftops to pick up more signals from Buffalo to provide a better color picture. This is what is happening on a number of community antenna systems today." He warned that unless the government acted, "Canada's centennial will be celebrated by black and white Canadian programs and by American color shows rebroadcast by the CBC and CTV networks."

As well as not encouraging Canadian television manufacturers by allowing color programming, the Canadian government had placed a severe tax burden on radio, TV and hi-fi products. In addition to an 11 percent manufacturers sales tax, consumers had to pay a 15 percent excise tax, originally imposed as a temporary wartime deterrent to luxury purchases.

A critical C.A. pointed out that these taxes were being applied differently to foreign-made products which gave them an unfair advantage over Canadian manufacturers. He cited the ludicrous possibility of Electrohome shipping products to the United States and then importing them back into Canada, where they could be sold at a lower price than if they had been sold through normal channels. His comments turned out to be an early warning signal of the death of the Canadian consumer electronics industry.

Some years later, his son, John—at the time representing the electronic consumer products trade association—was to tell a meeting of Ottawa deputy ministers that this practice was "the equivalent of self-imposed economic treason."

The company knew it was just a matter of time before the go-ahead was given to color and in 1965 proudly unveiled its own color TV chassis—the first to be made in Canada. Eleven models were introduced, priced from $795 to $1,895. Most were console models in a variety of furniture styles.

Circa 75's armchair had stereo speakers in wings. Console contains radio and record player.

Of major significance was the replacement of tubes with transistors, which Electrohome had pioneered in Canada after a study by Sydney F. Love, manager of engineering. Transistors were first used in Electrohome's 1964 black-and-white TV sets, one of which was an 11-inch portable which could be plugged into a car cigarette lighter.

Even though there were no color programs from Canadian TV stations, brisk sales were expected in communities where American color programs could be received, as well as exports to the United States.

In the same year, the company introduced its Circa 75 home entertainment package which featured high-backed leather easy chairs with built-in stereo speakers in the wings and audio and video controls in the armrests.

A specially-produced film linked the Circa 75 concept to the silver spheres of space satellites which by then were circling the globe. The film introduced such far-fetched ideas as satellite signals beaming TV programs from around the world for storage on "micro-tape and memory systems that will store program materials for playback at your leisure on giant wall screens." Another prediction was the use of two-way TV for shopping or telephone calls.

The heart of the Circa 75 system was a circular console, described as "a communications centre in your own living room." Conceived by product styling manager Gordon Duern, the Circa 75 embodied futuristic ideas that were to become reality over the ensuing 30 years and for Electrohome, provided a new focus for consumer electronic design for the following 10 years.

Despite ever-increasing sales and a continuously expanding list of products, C.A. expressed a note of caution which also turned out to contain a forecast of future problems. He told shareholders at the 1965 annual meeting:

"The potential in Canada makes us wish we could grow and expand faster than has been possible. However, we have learned some lessons and experience has taught us that too much diversification can become *divertification*—that moving too fast can be more trouble than the advancement is worth.

"Over the past 10 years we have placed a stronger emphasis on competent personnel, on research and development, on engineering, styling, production and latterly, our financial position. In this realm of growth, well thought-out corporate purposes can help keep a business ship on course."

C.A.'s drive to increase sales outside Canada continued to pay dividends. One area which was successfully targeted was the Caribbean and in 1966, Electrohome signed an agreement with a Jamaican company to make TV cabinets and assemble black and white TV sets.

In 1966, the Canadian government finally gave approval to Canadian color TV transmissions. As soon as colour telecasts began in September, sales began to pick up. To handle the anticipated surge in demand, color TV output was tripled. A 25,000 square foot, $400,000 addition was built on the Wellington Street plant and 75 more people were hired.

In the first eight months of 1967, Canadians bought 45,000 Electrohome color TV sets and by the end of the centennial year, sales of color TV sets had increased by 40 per cent over 1966.

On the company's 60th anniversary, shareholders approved a new name for the company, Electrohome Limited. The deletion of the "Dominion" reference was a reflection of the wave of national pride which swept through Canada during the 100th anniversary of Confederation.

The Centennial was celebrated in an atmosphere of prosperity and social change. Canadians argued the merits of a new Maple Leaf flag and were captivated by the charismatic style of then-Prime Minister Pierre Elliott Trudeau. At Expo 67 in Montreal, more than 80 Electrohome home entertainment products and Deilcraft furniture items were seen by tens of thousands of visitors from around the world who flocked to see the centennial world's fair.

Despite increased sales of color TV sets, Electrohome's overall revenue declined by $2.5 million in 1967, prompting Carl Pollock to blame government and labor for inflationary wage and salary increases which he said were causing unsettled conditions. He said wage increases as high as 20 per cent were not being matched by productivity gains and were hurting Canada's position in the export market.

But two years later, the last year of a decade which was to be labelled the Fabulous Sixties, it seemed as if the Golden Years were back again. Total sales reached $44.5 million—an increase of 25 per cent over 1968. And profits were $1.8 million, more than double the previous year and three times the figure for 1960.

In the previous 10 years, the number of employees had doubled to 2,248, making Electrohome the second largest employer in Kitchener-Waterloo, behind the Dominion Rubber Company. The original Amalgamated Workers Union had been replaced by two large international unions, the International Brotherhood of Electrical Workers and the Canadian Union of Operating Engineers.

The Profit Sharing Retirement Plan—long a symbol of excellent employee relations—had been discontinued

Deilcraft furniture displayed at Expo 67, the world's fair in Montreal celebrating Canada's 100th birthday.

with the introduction of the Canada Pension Plan and a new non-contributory retirement plan.

The company operated from 1.2 million square feet of space, including eight buildings in Kitchener and branch offices in Toronto, Winnipeg, Calgary and Vancouver.

Total sales had grown from $15.2 million in 1960 to $44.5 million in 1969. Almost every product line had shown substantial gains. Consumer electronic product sales had tripled and color television sales had gone from a nominal $17,000 in 1960 to be the largest single product line in 1969. Comfort appliance sales had experienced a seven-fold increase and furniture almost four-fold.

Sub-fractional horsepower motors, a staple of the company's industrial product line since the early 1930s, had shown an increase of more than three-fold over

In 1967, the 10 millionth small electric motor was made at Victoria Street plant.

the 1960 sales figure of $1 million. Division manager Seb Englert, who joined the company in 1943, had overseen the introduction of more than 400 different models that were being made at a rate of 10,000 motors a day. In addition to being used in many Electrohome products, they were used in car and truck heaters, kitchen and bathroom exhausts, oil burning stoves and space heaters, hot water heaters, refrigerators, air conditioners, sewing machines, movie projectors, emergency vehicle sirens, hair dryers, aquarium pumps and artificial hearts used by hospitals in heart operations. Among export markets were Sweden, Austria, West Germany New Zealand, France, Britain and the United States.

The technical products division, however, had not survived. Disappointing sales of the specialized equipment imported from manufacturers in Britain and the United States prompted the company to abandon this field in 1967.

One new market showing promise for the future was educational television. Receivers and monitors were being sold in increasing numbers to schools and universities across Canada. David Lowater, export sales manager, had developed the market by organizing a fleet of vans, each staffed by a technician and a teacher, to demonstrate the Electrohome Educator TV to school boards.

The organizers of the 1968 Olympic Games in Mexico City bought 800 educational sets and set them up in different areas of the city so that local people could watch the Games. Afterwards, the sets were donated by the Committee for on-going use in Mexico City schools.

Another offshoot of this market was the use of Electrohome monitors at conventions to broadcast speeches and allow delegates to watch business sessions from various convention locations. As well, monitors were being tested in 1969 at several Ontario racetracks, at several major airports, and in a few brokerage offices in the U.S. and Canada. Monitors were made for Trans-Lux in New York to replace large wall tickertape displays of changing stock prices. Brokers welcomed the opportunity to speak confidentially to their clients either on the telephone or in person from the privacy of their offices, referring to stock prices displayed on their own desktop monitor.

These products and the new markets being explored would play a significant role in the company's future directions.

Buoyed by the 1969 results and anticipating a continuation of prosperity, the company expanded its manufacturing capabilities even further. A 25,000 square foot addition was built onto the Wellington Street plant for color TV production. Even more significant was the acquisition of Honderich Industries Ltd. of Milverton and Fry and Blackhall Ltd. of Wingham, two old-established furniture manufacturers.

Harold Ruetz, who by this time had been promoted to general manager of the Deilcraft division, said the move "is in keeping with our long-term plans to broaden the base for furniture products under the Deilcraft name. It will further strengthen Deilcraft's growing position in the Canadian and export markets." Ruetz, who started with the Deilcraft division in 1951, held several managerial positions before returning to head the furniture operation when it moved to the large new plant in 1966.

In 1969, Clayton (Chunker) Allgeier died. He had started as an office boy with A.B. Pollock on Victoria Street and had risen to become a vice-president. In a tribute to his long service, C.A. said "he contributed much to our philosophy of good human relations."

The next generation of the Pollock family was represented by John Albon Pollock, C.A.'s only son, who in 1969 was made vice-president, electronic products, after working his way through several departments. He was

also elected to the board of directors and became a member of the corporate executive committee, which also included Howard Main, executive vice-president, marketing and public relations; Donald S. Sykes, executive vice-president, finance and corporate relations, Harold I. Eby, secretary-treasurer; and C.A. Pollock.

The other members of the management team heading into the 1970s were: Gordon L. Duern, director of design; Bernard F. Ellis, general sales manager, electronic products; Seb Englert, general manager, motor division; Ronald R. Freuere, general manager, product planning, contract, export electronic products division; Ron W. Johnson, general manager, appliance division; Dave H. Johnston, general manager of engineering and manufacturing, electronic products; Maurice G. Monteith, general manager, industrial relations.

In 1969, American astronaut Neil Armstrong set foot on the moon. Crowds gathered at Speakers Corner in downtown Kitchener to watch the event on specially-installed Electrohome color TV sets. They heard him make his now-famous pronouncement: "That's one small step for a man, one giant leap for mankind."

That same year, Carl Pollock looked ahead "to a future that includes expansion, consolidation and diversification." He acknowledged the existence of some clouds on the economic horizon but his optimism was unshaken. It was obvious that he and his team were looking forward to a giant leap forward for Electrohome.

John A. Pollock, third generation of founding family, joined board of directors in 1969.

CHAPTER SEVEN

1970-1980 Fighting for Survival

Large screen colour TV projectors (opposite) introduced in the 1970s, were the forerunner of today's visual communications business segment.

Futuristic "bubble" stereo (right), featured award-winning metal spinning technique developed by Electrohome engineers.

The growth and expansion forecast by Carl Pollock at the end of the Sixties continued into the 1970s. But the optimism of the Electrohome team was about to be severely tested. After four years of record-setting sales through 1970-74, the company was abruptly brought to its knees, its workforce cut in half and its very survival in doubt.

The cause of this dramatic downturn in Electrohome's fortunes was a worldwide recession at a time when the company had embarked on a course of expansion which left it financially vulnerable. The situation was described in one magazine article as being caught in a "down" market while in the middle of an "up" cycle and expanding aggressively.

Plans for expansion were made at the beginning of the 1970s when Canadians were still in a spending mood and were buying television sets, stereo receivers and furniture at a record-setting pace. The mood was buoyant as the company looked forward to a continuation of the growth pattern of the Sixties.

The first move was the acquisition in 1970 of Central Ontario Television Ltd., with the objective of widening Electrohome's interests in the communications industry. The company, owned equally by Carl Pollock and Famous Players, was bought by Electrohome for $4.3 million in cash and shares.

The TV station came on the market because of a

Electrohome bought CKCO-TV from Carl Pollock in 1970. The station is still operating from the same location on King Street West in Kitchener.

clause in the Broadcasting Act against foreign ownership of communications companies. Because Famous Players was controlled by Gulf and Western of the United States, the Canadian Radio-Television and Telecommunications Commission (CRTC) ruled that Famous Players was not eligible to own Central Ontario Television. The directive triggered the sale of Famous Players shares to C.A., who in turn sold all the shares in the company to Electrohome.

The television station and its sister radio stations, CKKW-AM and CFCA-FM, were placed under the control of a newly-created subsidiary, Electrohome Communications Ltd., which was set up for the purpose of permitting a public stock issue of shares while still leaving controlling interest with Electrohome. W.D. (Bill) McGregor, vice-president and general manager of Central Ontario Television, joined the Electrohome team.

The 1964 acquisition of CKKW-AM had allowed

Carl Pollock to finally achieve his goal of owning a successful radio station. The station was started in 1959 by a former CKCO-TV news director, Alan Hodge, who convinced several local businessmen to provide financial backing. Hodge died suddenly in 1962 from a heart attack while attending a Rotary Club meeting. Two years later, C.A. bought the station and moved it from the Dunker Building in downtown Kitchener to the CKCO-TV site at 864 King St. West. In 1966, Carl Pollock re-applied for an FM licence and a year later, CFCA went on the air with 100,000 watts of power. The opening ceremonies included a live broadcast of a concert by the K-W Symphony with Frederick Pohl conducting.

The broadcasting operations had enjoyed steadily-increasing advertising revenues and had consistently earned a profit in the highly-competitive southwestern Ontario market. These profits were to play a major role in Electrohome's survival later in the decade.

Soon after the change in ownership, CKCO launched the first in a series of expansion moves with the opening of a re-broadcasting station at Wiarton to send CKCO's signals throughout the Georgian Bay area, which was expected to increase advertising revenues from this pre-dominantly vacation area.

By 1975, CKCO-TV had added transmitters at Huntsville and Wallaceburg to expand

Opening of CKCO's Wallaceburg transmitter featured (left to right) Chatham Mayor Douglas G. Allin; Carl Pollock; and Sarnia Mayor Andy Brandt.

its coverage to all of southwestern and central northern Ontario, which opened up additional audience and advertising markets. In addition, CKKW had moved to a new broadcasting frequency and built a new transmitter at Ayr, south of Kitchener. Nine 500-foot towers boosted signal power from 1,000 to 10,000 watts and increased the station's coverage area to reach a population of 1.2 million.

Stylish occasional tables like these contributed to a 50 per cent increase in Deilcraft furniture sales in 1972.

During this period, the company's broadcasting successes were being matched by every other business segment. In 1972, for example, furniture sales increased by 50 per cent. Every year there was a new sales record—from $51.2 million in 1970 to $69.7 million in 1971 and to $88 million in 1972. And in 1973, sales went over the $100 million mark for the first time, with profits at close to $3.3 million, another record.

The company embarked on a series of moves designed to satisfy the demand for products. Every division was involved.

A 50 per cent increase in furniture sales in 1972 brought expansion on several fronts. Two Stratford furniture manufacturers were acquired, Flexsteel Industries (Canada) Ltd., which specialized in quality upholstered and contract furniture, and Fairfield Furniture Industries Ltd., a maker of occasional chairs. Another 130,000 square feet was added to the Deilcraft furniture plant in Kitchener's southwest industrial park and equipment installed to allow the company to make molded plastic components, finished to look like wood, for the home furnishings field.

Of greater significance was the purchase of a large woodworking plant in Stellarton, N.S., built by Clairtone, a competitor in the home entertainment field run by entrepreneurs Peter Munk and David Gilmour. The plant was intended to capitalize on increased demand for stereo consoles but this Nova Scotia expansion contributed to Clairtone's subsequent bankruptcy. Electrohome bought the 256,000 square foot plant from the Nova Scotia government, to make an expanded line of bedroom furniture. The promise of job creation attracted a grant from the federal Department of Regional Economic Expansion.

An 87,000 square foot addition to the Wellington Street electronics plant was built to take care of the high demand for color TV sets and stereo components. One of the company's best customers still was the T. Eaton Company, for whom Electrohome made Viking brand home entertainment products. Another major "private brand" client was the U.S. retail giant, Sears, Roebuck & Co., which bought substantial quantities of a unique

Electrohome's leadership in home entertainment products continued in 1973 with the introduction of the four-channel stereo.

type of year-round air conditioning product which combined the functions of both a humidifier and dehumidifier.

At a dealer meeting in 1973, the company unveiled more than 60 new products, including four-channel stereo and a new line of turntables and other components. The big news was the introduction of a "super module" color TV chassis which could be replaced in the customer's home in minutes. Dealers were proudly told that in terms of product quality, Electrohome was rated by the Consumers Association of Canada second only to Zenith products from the United States.

To reduce the company's reliance on outside sources of supply, a manufacturer of printed circuit boards was acquired, Lightning Circuits of Niagara-on-the-Lake.

With the same objective in mind, it was decided to establish a factory in a duty free area of Kuala Lumpur, Malaysia, to manufacture electronic chassis for television sets, some of which the company had been buying from other Far East suppliers. David H. Johnston, general manager of engineering and manufacturing for electronic products, was made president and general manager of a newly-formed subsidiary, Electrohome Malaysia, and given the responsibility for getting the plant up and running.

Another major move was to create separate manufacturing facilities for small motors, which by then was spread over three Kitchener locations. A 125,000 square foot plant employing 350 was built in nearby Cambridge, which increased production capacity for future growth.

The removal of small motor production from Victoria Street provided much-needed space for the appliance division to meet a seemingly endless demand for air moving appliances such as fans, humidifiers and dehumidifiers, air purifiers, and baseboard heaters.

Air conditioners were made for Electrohome by KeepRite in Brantford and were the best-selling brand in Canada.

Air moving appliances can still be found in households today.

The consumer service division headed by Herb LaPier moved to its own building on Weber Street North in Waterloo and acted as the central service point and headquarters for the company's 11 branches and scores of franchised outlets across the country.

To capitalize on the acceptance in Europe of Electrohome TV monitors, the company established a

sales office at Herne Bay in Kent, England. It was the marketing base for Britain and Europe for commercial and electronic products. The move was seen as the start of a six-year program that would include establishing manufacturing and warehousing facilities in Europe.

The picture was indeed rosy and the Electrohome team was demonstrating its confidence in a number of other ways. One was the opening of a permanent furniture showroom at the Toronto International Centre to showcase Deilcraft and Flexsteel products. The other was the co-sponsorship with the Canadian government of a series of lectures on the importance of design, held at universities across Canada, with Carl Pollock as host.

The company's successes drove up the price of shares on the Toronto Stock Exchange. *The Kitchener-Waterloo Record* noted that Electrohome stock doubled in price from January to September of 1972, and was ranked 56th among most actively traded stocks. In June 1972, shareholders benefitted from a five for one stock split.

By 1972, Carl Pollock had handed over more responsibility to his son, John, who was then vice-president, electronic products. He became president while his father remained chairman of the board. John Pollock called 1972 the most dynamic year in the company's history. The number of employees rose by 36 per cent

to 3,400 working in 1,596,000 square feet of factories, offices and service areas.

Despite the good news, C.A.'s analytical mind had seen storm signals on the horizon. He commented that the 1970s "are proving to be times of radical change. The international and domestic economic environments are beset by inflation, unemployment and mounting taxes," which he blamed on "the questionable stimulants of increasing prices and expanded government spending, the circulation of added monies, and the hope that somehow our problems will resolve themselves." A constant theme was the weakening of Canadian manufacturing by low-cost imports from the United States and the Far East.

In November 1972, the company was hit by a three-week strike—the first in the company's history—which affected the company's performance well into 1973. A saddened Carl Pollock said: "We have always considered our relations with our member employees as a partnership."

Sales continued at a record-setting pace in 1973—up 22 per cent to $107 million—but net income dropped by 26 per cent to $3.3 million from $4.5 million in 1972. And at the annual meeting held in the spring of 1974, C.A. told shareholders to expect more bad news. While sales in the first quarter of 1974 were ahead of the previous year's pace, profit levels would not be maintained because of continuing unsettled economic conditions.

This was C.A.'s final appearance as board chairman. On May 15, 1974, at age 70, he announced his retirement from the company after 45 years of active—some might

Donald S. Sykes (seated, left), took over as chairman in 1974 following C.A.'s (seated right) retirement. Standing are John A. Pollock (left), president; and Howard W. Main, executive vice-president, who was also chairman of Central Ontario Television Ltd.

say intense—involvement in leading the company. His place as chairman was taken by Donald S. Sykes, who had started with the company in 1947 as an accountant and in 27 years had become secretary-treasurer and later executive vice-president. Sykes also became chairman of the executive committee. The other members of the senior team were John Pollock and Howard W. Main, executive vice-president and chairman of the board of directors of Central Ontario Television Ltd.

The new Electrohome team could not possibly have foreseen just how bad things were going to get.

There were encouraging figures for the first nine months of 1974—an overall increase in sales of 9.2 per cent. But in October, when consumer goods sales usually began to increase in the runup to Christmas, there was a noticeable drop-off in orders. The decline became more pronounced as each month passed. In the last three months of 1974, sales declined by 20.4 per cent, wiping out the earlier increases.

The bottom had fallen out of the marketplace. Electrohome was caught with massive inventories and overhead costs geared to the expansionary philosophy of the past few years.

Profits plummeted from $3.3 million in 1973 to a meagre $147,000 a year later. That was just the beginning.

Between 1975 and 1977, the company lost $11.7 million. The price of Electrohome shares on the Toronto Stock Exchange—as high as $21 in 1972—went as low as $1.72 in 1977.

A subsequent analysis by *Executive* magazine said the suddenness of the drop in sales overwhelmed the company. The article quoted John Pollock: "In the early 1970s, color television was in a boom period in Canada, while our second most important product, furniture, was going through substantial expansion. Regrettably, both these businesses fell out of bed at the same time."

There were numerous contributing factors: The rapid growth of domestic color TV in the early 1970s masked an increasingly difficult and competitive environment. As early as 1971, John Pollock had headed an industry-wide review which challenged the sale of imported television products at prices lower than in their domestic markets. John was then president of the consumer products division of the Electronic Industries Association.

A government-appointed tribunal found that there had been "injurious dumping" and assessed duties against the importers. But the decision was successfully appealed on a technicality and the tribunal findings were overturned. This opened the door to even more offshore imports, threatening the future of Canadian manufacturers.

In 1973, Electrohome found itself the sole remaining Canadian-owned company in the electronics manufacturing and marketing business in Canada. The company had to compete against 50 Japanese companies, 18 from the United States, five from Germany, three from Britain, two from Denmark and one from France.

In the same year, the Organization of Petroleum Exporting Countries (OPEC) created tidal waves in the world economy by drastically increasing oil prices. The cost of crude oil from the Middle East rose by more than 120 per cent from April to October.

Around the world, inflation sent prices skyrocketing. Price and wage controls were imposed by the Canadian government in 1975. Pay increases were limited by an Anti-Inflation Board to 8 per cent. The result was a major worldwide recession. People stopped buying houses and consumer goods—or looked for cheaper products.

Canadians were outraged at the skyrocketing price for the 1976 Olympic Games held in Montreal. Opened by Queen Elizabeth II, the games cost $1.5 billion. In the same year, the Toronto Blue Jays took to the field and Rene Levesque's Parti Quebecois gained power in Quebec.

The overturned anti-dumping decision of 1971 came back to haunt Canadian manufacturers. American furniture manufacturers exported their surplus inventory to Canada at bargain basement prices, at the expense of Canadian furniture manufacturers including Deilcraft. The Japanese did the same with cut-price home entertainment products, particularly television sets. Non-consumer products made by Electrohome were similarly affected.

In this rapidly-changing environment, Electrohome found it all but impossible to compete.

As John Pollock repeatedly pointed out, the competition was unfair. Canadian firms paid higher wages and benefits than foreign competitors and were also saddled with an onerous level of manufacturing tax, which resulted in domestic manufacturers paying more in taxes than competing imports.

Within this framework, Electrohome found itself seriously over-extended. Over $3 million in unsold television products and components had to be written off. If TV and other home entertainment products were no longer viable, the company needed to invest in new opportunities. But this required substantial commitment to new engineering capacity—and working capital was in a deficit position.

The company approached the federal government's Enterprise Development Board (EDB) for loan guarantees to finance this new area of expansion. The EDB commissioned an international management consulting firm to conduct a business analysis. The consultant's report sounded alarm bells for the company's bankers, the Royal Bank of Canada.

According to *Executive* magazine, the company's financial position "was serious enough to raise doubts in the minds of staff, suppliers and customers whether

Fierce competition from off-shore TV manufacturers in the mid-1970s prompted advertisements like this one, created for Electrohome dealers who inserted their own 'sale' prices.

Electrohome would be able to stay in business at all." Intense negotiations followed between the EDB, the Royal Bank and the company. Carl Pollock came out of retirement to get involved, along with his friend, Walter A. Bean, deputy chairman and vice-president of Canada Trust and a member of the Electrohome board since 1954.

The result was a 15-year loan for $25 million from the Royal Bank, of which $15 million was insured by the EDB. The company had to provide the EDB with an option to buy 436,000 Electrohome shares at their current value, $2.06. This option was to provide a significant windfall for the government three years later.

As another condition of the loan, Electrohome agreed to the appointment in late 1976 of a new chairman and chief executive officer, James Holmes, a former vice-president of finance with Falconbridge Mines Ltd. and a director of financial planning and treasurer of Canadian Pacific Ltd. Carl Pollock became honorary chairman. In addition, D.W. Morrison, a retired banker, was appointed to represent the Royal Bank. They replaced Mrs. Carl Pollock and Donald R. Steele, husband of Carl's daughter, Barbara. The resignation of Mr. Steele, a long-time board member, coincided with his appointment as an Ontario Supreme Court judge.

A few months later, following non-payment of dividends on preferred shares in 1977, holders of these shares elected two members to the board, George S. Dembroski and Lee W. Larkin. J.M. Bridgman, representing the EDB, was also elected to the board at the annual meeting held in the spring of 1978. At this point, the company had a 10-member board—the biggest in its history—of which six represented outside interests.

To provide Holmes with as much help as possible, the board of directors met monthly instead of the customary three or four times a year. Holmes reported weekly to the Royal Bank and the EDB. He also met weekly with Walter Bean, whose lifetime of business and community service experience provided a valuable perspective on Electrohome's history and corporate culture.

Holmes found that the Electrohome management team had already taken the first steps toward restoring profitability.

An example was a decision to abandon TV manufacturing. A Canadian government ruling late in 1976 allowed Canadian manufacturers to import television sets duty free in direct proportion to the value of their Canadian production of eligible electronic products. Hard on the heels of the ruling, Electrohome found a willing partner in The Victor Company of Japan, Limited (JVC). Established in 1927, JVC had a reputation for product quality and outstanding engineering. A 10-year agreement was signed under which Electrohome would import JVC television chassis to be installed in Electrohome-made products.

Holmes negotiated a new financing relationship for these imports with JVC, its trading company, Kanematsu-Gosho, and its bankers. A major benefit was that Electrohome was not required to pay in advance for its purchases, as was the historic Japanese practice.

The JVC contract led to a reduction of in-house manufacturing levels of consumer electronic products. The vacant space at the Wellington Street plant was taken over by the Service Division and the division's Weber Street building in Waterloo was sold. Appliance manufacturing was also moved into the Wellington Street plant from the old multi-floor Plant 1 at Duke and Breithaupt Street—the original furniture plant—which, also was sold.

The Flexsteel upholstered furniture plant in Stratford was sold. Woodworking plants in Wingham and New Hamburg were shut down and sold. The Hawkesville sawmill and lumber plant was closed. The huge plant in Stellarton, N.S. which lost $3 million and never really reached its full potential, was another casualty. Thanks to some letter-of-the-law bureaucrats in Ottawa, this particular closing cost Electrohome a $1 million penalty. Financial support from the federal government to buy the plant had been conditional on Electrohome providing employment for a specified period. The plant was closed two months before the contract expired and despite the company's protests that it had upheld the spirit of the agreement, the government insisted on extracting a penalty.

"They nailed us to the wall," said a rueful John Pollock. "We could have kept a couple of watchmen on for another two months and not had to pay the $1 million."

The innovative venture in Kuala Lumpur was closed down in 1977. Despite building up a workforce as high as 400, the increasing pace of technological change and long delivery cycles reduced any advantage the plant had. Coupled with the rapid erosion of the Canadian market, the plant became redundant.

These cuts brought about a corresponding reduction in the company's workforce. From a high of 4,400 in 1972, the payroll plunged to 1,900 in 1978.

The injection of working capital and reductions in staff and operations had staved off disaster. By late 1978, the company was on the road to recovery. A profit of $156,000 was announced for the third quarter, compared with a loss of $779,000 for the same period the year before. Inventory levels had decreased from a high of $43.7 million in 1974 to $19.8 million in 1978.

Following a satisfying fourth quarter, an overall profit of $709,000 was announced—the first in three years. By this time, the oil crisis recession had ended and exchange rates were again favoring Canadian companies.

The key element in Electrohome's turnaround had been the acceptance of the "new order" in consumer electronics.

Electrohome had joined such household names as General Electric, Philco, Admiral and Fleetwood in

In the mid-Seventies, Electrohome's survival strategy included importing color TV chassis from Japan and mounting them in Deilcraft console cabinets like this.

withdrawing from the complete manufacture of TV sets. Instead, they imported chassis made by companies in Japan, Taiwan, Singapore and Korea, and using Canadian-made picture tubes and other components, assembled them in Electrohome cabinets. There were no fully-integrated Canadian companies left and only a handful of U.S. manufacturers including RCA and Zenith.

The disastrous middle years of the 1970s had made it clear that Electrohome would have to abandon its vision as a Canadian-based consumer electronics manufacturer that could compete with the industry giants around the world. The new strategy meant, as John Pollock described it later, "broadening our products and markets while reducing our historic dependence on the cyclical consumer area. These changes were coupled with the need to strengthen our ability to manage new economic realities."

One major move was to establish a separate consumer electronic marketing division. Howard Main, executive vice-president, took on the additional responsibility for marketing all Electrohome consumer products including imported television and other home entertainment products and a number of new products including increasingly-popular microwave ovens.

Microwave ovens were among many consumer products which replaced the manufacture of TV sets.

This allowed the electronics division to concentrate on commercial and industrial products such as specialized video monitors for surveillance systems, stock exchange and brokerage trading floors and broadcasting stations. The company won a $1.3 million contract from IBM to supply data display monitors and was involved in developing consumer and commercial applications for the Canadian government's Telidon video information systems.

The Advent large-screen color TV projection system led Electrohome into a profitable new business venture.

Another area which showed great promise was large-screen color TV projection. In a move which was to have significant long-term repercussions, Electrohome's Don Harrold visited Henry Kloss, a physicist and engineer who was president of Advent Corporation of Cambridge, Mass., across the street from the Massachusetts Institute of Technology. Harrold's interest had been aroused by a magazine article describing Advent's projection system. He saw an opportunity to use some of the large inventory of TV components left when

Electrohome stopped making consumer television sets. Harrold came away from the meeting with Kloss with a $4.5 million contract under which the electronics for all Advent products would be designed and made by Electrohome and integrated with Advent optics.

Strong sales were anticipated as consumers discovered the impact of what was described as "life-size television." Although numerous sales of the large-screen systems were made to bars, taverns, clubs and other public locations, the product's high price limited its appeal for consumers. Electrohome's pioneering efforts were joined later by Japanese manufacturers which increased competition and made the market less attractive.

The U.S. company subsequently experienced financial difficulties and Henry Kloss lost control. But Electrohome's original contract included the right to make and sell large screen projection systems based on Advent designs anywhere in the world. This contract—and the specialized knowledge of a new market gained from the Advent relationship—was to lead the company into a new and profitable market, commercial data projection systems.

The search for a more diversified product line led the company into several new fields, or adaptations of previous areas of expertise. The company's service department, for example, which operated coast-to-coast, obtained computer maintenance contracts for mini-computers in restaurant chains, stock exchange communication systems, airport reservation systems and other industrial applications. The division's familiarity with complex systems led to the design of closed circuit tele-vision surveillance systems for commercial, industrial and institutional customers.

At the metal fabricating plant on Victoria Street in Kitchener, the company's energy conservation research laboratories, in co-operation with the University of Waterloo, worked on the development of products in the fields of solar energy and waste heat recovery.

Another high-tech area was the development of reverse osmosis/ultrafiltration systems to provide pure water supplies required by painting, metalworking and food processing companies.

The search for new products resulted in the development of a reverse osmosis water filtration system.

The equipment engineering group at the Wellington Street plant, no longer involved in supporting TV set manufacturing, was facing the prospect of laying off several of its highly skilled engineers. Doug Wismer, manager of equipment engineering, convinced his boss, Jim Washburn, that he could find new outlets for their expertise and bring in enough additional revenue to

You know what they say about the Mounties.

"They always get their man." That's the reputation of the Royal Canadian Mounted Police. And it's what people are also saying about another famous Canadian outfit. Electrohome.

Electrohome is Canada's leading television manufacturer, with a 68-year reputation for excellence in electronics. Like all Electrohome products, our CCTV monitors are built to some very particular standards of performance and reliability. What's more, they're priced particularly low. Choose 9", 11" or 23" screens in metal cabinets or rack mounts.

Warehouse, bank, plant, apartment — whatever you're monitoring, you can count on Electrohome CCTV. Every time.

Just like the Mounties.

For a brochure, and information on our surprisingly low prices, write Electrohome Limited 919 N. Michigan Avenue Chicago, Illinois 60611

ELECTROHOME

Electrohome monitors were used in surveillance systems installed in department stores, as depicted in this advertisement.

more than justify keeping them on as members of the team. Their efforts resulted in a number of projects for other companies, ranging from electronic testing equipment destined for the Soviet Union to an electronic scanner to measure the bacteria count in hot dogs.

It also resulted in the company finding a new field—monitors for video games—that to the surprise of some company sceptics, was to prove successful.

It started with a contract to make black-and-white monitors for a new type of computerized "ping-pong" video game being made by a Toronto firm. The contract allowed Electrohome to use components left over from TV manufacturing operations. Unfortunately, the Toronto customer ran out of money, according to Doug Wismer, leaving Electrohome with 200 ping-pong games. These were eventually sold to a buyer in Greece. "We lost money but we learned a lot about the video game business," Wismer later recalled.

He spent the next three years getting acquainted with manufacturers and researching their requirements. "The design engineers were pleasantly surprised to have a big manufacturer like Electrohome offering to build

monitors to their own specifications. In the past, they had bought consumer TV sets, stripped them down and used the parts they needed."

At first, black and white monitors were made for most of the games manufacturers as the company's name and reputation for quality spread around the industry. The introduction of color monitors for games was not to occur until the early 1980s, with significant benefits for Electrohome.

The diversification program continued during 1979 with successful results. Overall sales increased by 31 per cent to $128.7 million—a new high. And profit rose markedly to $3.4 million.

Each business segment—industrial, consumer, service and communications— had sales increases and each operated at a profit.

Despite these encouraging signs, John Pollock and his management team were not happy with the large fees and high loan costs the company was paying to its bankers. Donald Sykes found an alternative in the Toronto-Dominium Bank, which had built up expertise in the broadcasting field through a business relationship with Rogers Cable. According to one industry observer, the T-D Bank was ahead of other major banks in recognizing opportunities for growth in broadcasting and was the first to accept cash flow generated by cable TV subscribers as a measure of financial strength instead of the traditional asset base.

A proposal from the T-D bank, containing signifi-

The company had a brief but profitable involvement in the video game business, starting with this VideoSport coin-operated hockey or tennis game.

cantly more favorable terms, was accepted by the Electrohome board. The company switched its long-term debt to the T-D, retiring the EDB-insured portion. The Royal Bank was left with the smaller operating loan business which a year later, was turned over to the Bank of Nova Scotia.

This action triggered the departure in mid-1979 of James Holmes, whose contract was not renewed after he declared that his mission had been accomplished. At the next annual meeting, the Royal Bank's representative, D.W. Morrison, was not re-elected.

John Pollock moved from president to the position of chairman and vice-president of operations and Stewart Maclellan, an accountant with a strong background in industrial products, became president and chief executive officer. Donald Sykes continued as executive vice-president and two executives were named vice-presidents: Herbert H. LaPier, general manager of the electronics division, and Bill McGregor, president of CAP Communications (the new name for Central Ontario Television).

By the time the 1980 results were in, the nightmare appeared to be well and truly over.

Sales had shot up by 43 per cent to $184 million and income more than doubled to $9.5 million. For the first time since 1977, a dividend was paid on preference shares, prompting the retirement of two directors representing preference shareholders, G.S. Dembroski and L.W. Larkin.

Dembroski, vice-chairman and director of RBC Dominion Securities Inc., subsequently rejoined the board in 1981. J.W. Bridgman, originally elected to represent the EDB, had become a strong supporter of Electrohome management and continued to serve. They were joined by S.A. Wilgar of Warner-Lambert and William Moeser, a retired Kitchener manufacturing executive. All four brought valuable industrial experience to advise John Pollock in the ensuing years. (Wilgar was transferred to the United States and was replaced in 1982 by Robert J. Collins-Wright, president and chief executive officer of Inglis Limited).

As result of the return to profitability, the price of Electrohome shares shot up as high as $38. The EDB took advantage of the increase by selling the shares pledged for its loan and made a windfall profit of $11.3 million. The company could have bought the shares back—but would have needed another loan to do it!

One of the most significant results of the diversification program was the diminishing importance and proportion of consumer products—now contributing only about 40 per cent of total sales—and an even smaller proportion of profits.

Both CAP Communications and the industrial division were far more profitable. The electronic division's aggressive search for new business opportunities had resulted in several notable successes.

One was a new large screen monochrome data projection system which interfaced with most computers.

Electrohome scored a world first with this product, a spinoff from the original Advent large screen TV system. Terry Schmidt, one of the company's creative engineers, conceived the idea of using a specialized monochrome

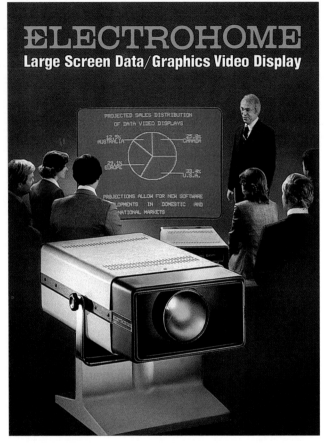

ELECTROHOME
Large Screen Data/Graphics Video Display

Electrohome scored a world first with this large-screen monochrome data/graphics video display.

tube to achieve an unprecedented level of brightness. It was the first of a series of pioneering developments which was to position Electrohome as a world leader in this field.

Customers included the New York and Chicago commodity exchanges. Innovative video products and systems for the computer and word processing industries were being sold in several overseas markets. Electrohome also pioneered the development of Telidon display terminals based on the Canadian government's unique videotex system.

The industrial products division still dominated the domestic market for sub-fractional motors, made for large volume manufacturers of automotive, commercial vehicle, consumer and comfort appliance products. By this time, Seb Englert had retired and had been replaced by Herb LaPier, who invited David Lowater to launch a major marketing effort to attract more export business. The move paid off—about

Sub-fractional motors were sold to many domestic manufacturers and exported to over 20 countries.

65 per cent of all motors made went to customers in 20 countries. The company's flexibility in being able to custom-design motors for a customer's specific application was a major factor in the division's success. New areas of business included all-purpose DC fans, marine bilge blowers, rear window defoggers, barbecue rotisseries and roof vent kits for recreational vehicles.

The Cambridge plant's plastic manufacturing capabilities were attracting orders ranging from computer terminal housings to decorative furniture facings. One unique application was the production of flotation collars to contain oil spills.

New markets were being developed for metal stampings in the automotive, appliance and electronic fields. Environmental systems had moved beyond the treatment of soluble oil and water waste into the design of other ultrafiltration products. The food processing industry was among several which recognized the cost reduction, energy saving and waste control benefits offered by this technology. Printed circuit boards made at the Niagara-on-the-Lake plant were being bought by a growing number of new customers including several in the automotive industry.

A significant increase in income had resulted from a Canadian government duty remission program which had made it cost-effective to return the assembly of color TV sets to the Wellington Street plant. The electronics group, in addition to retail sales of home entertainment products, was selling large screen projection color TVs and specially-made color sets to hotels and motels.

The furniture group, buoyed by an Ontario Government Trillium Award for an occasional table collection, had introduced stylish new designs in occasional tables and new bedroom and dining suites. And

In the late 1970s, Electrohome continued diversifying with many new products like this electronic bug lantern.

the appliance group, while expanding its market share for air conditioners, humidifiers, dehumidifiers and fans, had added several new products including electronic bug lanterns.

By 1980, the company's broadcasting interests had become a major force in Ontario. CKCO-TV was broadcasting to two million viewers each week from stations in Kitchener, Wallaceburg, Wiarton and Huntsville. The station's local news service had been converted to electronic news gathering equipment and produced over 25

Stylish new designs in dining suites were introduced by Deilcraft in the late 1970s.

hours a week of local programming. Some of this was supplied to the CTV network with which it was affiliated.

A full-scale upgrading of production, programming, news and technical facilities got under way in 1980 at a cost of $2.2 million. Despite vying for audience share in the most competitive area in Canada, CKCO and its radio affiliates, CKKW-AM and CFCA-FM, were attracting a loyal base of viewers. To supplement revenue from the sale of advertising air time, CAP Communications was actively engaged in the sale and production of radio and TV commercials for a variety of clients.

The upsurge in business had brought a steady increase in the workforce. From the low point of 1,900 in 1978, the number of employees went from 2,418 in 1979 to 2,561 in 1980—still a long way from the 4,400 "members" working for the company in 1972. Five

union labor contracts were ratified in 1980 providing average increases including fringe benefits of 11-12 per cent, an indication of the annual cost-of-living increases that were normal at the time.

In the midst of the rollercoaster ride through the Seventies, Electrohome lost more than money. It lost the contribution of Carl Pollock, who died suddenly on August 16, 1978, after a heart attack at his Muskoka cottage, at the age of 74. The 1978 annual report said: "His leadership and achievements in a career that spanned 49 years with the company, were legend to Canadians in many walks of life. Mr. Pollock remained active in the company until the time of his death and his contributions will be sorely missed." His daughter, Barbara Steele, a substantial shareholder, joined the board to represent her family's financial interests.

Another major contributor to the company's growth and success, Howard Main, died in 1980. John Pollock paid tribute to the significant contributions he made in design and marketing during his 45-year career.

In the course of a tumultuous decade, Electrohome had gone from a large-scale manufacturer of home entertainment products and furniture, fighting to stay alive in a marketplace in which it could no longer compete, to become a manufacturer of specialty products and an emerging force in high-tech electronics and communications.

Its leaders had come through the dark tunnel of disaster and emerged on the other side, wiser and more focussed on their destiny.

The successful reversal of Electrohome's fortunes enabled John Pollock to look to the future with confidence. He told shareholders, employees, suppliers and customers: "Future prospects for the company are favorable. We believe that growth potential exists in each business segment and that a firm foundation has been established for continued progress."

Carl A. Pollock:
A Man Who Loved Canada

Carl Pollock often said he was not anti-American— "I'm pro-Canadian."

His message always was that Canadians can do anything they want to do "and I think they can do it better than anyone else, provided they want to." In a 1974 tribute on the occasion of his retirement from the company, the *Kitchener-Waterloo Record* said: "Some might see this as excessively chauvinistic, but still it contains a basic truth which Canadians have needed to acknowledge and act on. The fact that more Canadians are now realizing the validity of the message is due in substantial measure to the example of men like Carl Pollock."

As a young man, Carl Pollock was a keen athlete. But like everything else he did, he was not content until he had excelled. While a graduate student at Oxford University, he rowed against the Cambridge University team in the famous annual race on the River Thames. He also ran for the Oxford track team.

His first career choice was to become a university professor and after returning from Oxford, he taught for a short time in the department of aeronautical engineering at the University of Toronto. But when family ties called, he joined his father, A.B. Pollock, and brought to his business career the same intense level of commitment that won him places on the University teams and numerous academic honors.

In 1969, when he received his pin to commemorate 40 years with the company, a newspaper report said: "He still calls on his dealers in 22 countries around the world and when time permits, relaxes by walking, listening to good music, boating—and being with good people." He often worked 14-hour days and

Carl, always busy with speaking engagements, addresses a CKCO press conference.

was frequently in his office on Sundays. On one such weekend, he triggered an alarm which he couldn't turn off and had to explain who he was when the police arrived to investigate.

His son, John, described his father as "a very creative individual who could see a bigger picture than most of us and was always looking for new avenues to explore."

Despite the self-discipline that made him a successful scholar, athlete and businessman, he had his little weaknesses. He liked to smoke but fought a lifelong battle with himself against the habit. There were legions of Electrohome employees who had received a nickel (or more as the price increased) from C.A. for the cigarette he'd cadged from them.

John Pollock again:

"C.A. considered Electrohome as family. Whatever happened to Electrohome, happened to him. He gave the company heart and conscience and character.

"His father, A.B., was a numbers man, who didn't really get his hands dirty. C.A. did everything and knew everybody personally. He was a warm caring person."

These traits are illustrated by C.A.'s lifelong habit of sending postcards containing a simple greeting to plant workers, customers, friends, business colleagues. It was his way of staying in touch. Donald Sykes, who worked with C.A. for over 25 years, told of a business trip he took with C.A. to New York.

"We travelled by train and when it came time to return, we headed for Grand Central Station. There, I had a sandwich because our meeting had gone on for so long that we had had nothing to eat. When I looked up, C.A. was busy writing postcards. His sandwich was left untouched."

Electrohome attracted take-over offers from time-to-time, mainly from U.S. firms who saw the company as a threat, according to Sykes.

One such company sent a representative to see C.A., with orders to buy Electrohome. C.A. told him he wasn't interested. The American said, "Everyone has a price, what's yours?" C.A. told him the company was not for sale and asked him to leave.

His interests ranged far and wide, despite a work schedule that many would regard as punishing.

Although he abandoned his original goal of becoming a university professor, he

C.A. says good-bye to his wife, Helen, outside their Kitchener home.

rubbed shoulders with the academic world throughout his life. He was one of the founders of the University of Waterloo and worked diligently with engineering dean Dr. Douglas T. Wright to establish the co-operative education programs for which the university became famous. Electrohome was one of the first companies to accept students enrolled in co-op engineering. He was an active fund-raiser for the university and served as chairman of the board of governors and later chancellor. Dr. Wright, subsequently president of the university, later became an Electrohome director.

As president of the Canadian Manufacturers Association, he made dozens of speeches from Tokyo to St. John's, Newfoundland. He was called the association's most energetic leader. He was also a governor of the Ontario Research Foundation, past president of the Electronic Industries Association of Canada, the Ontario Chamber of Commerce and the Ontario Design Council.

His interest in the arts led him to become a founding member of the Stratford Festival and a director of the Kitchener-Waterloo Symphony. He was also a strong supporter of the proposal to build an arts centre in Kitchener which became The Centre in the Square.

In addition to being president of Electrohome, he was president of Central Ontario Television Ltd., vice-president and director of A. and C. Boehmer Ltd., director of Burns Foods Ltd., the Royal Bank of Canada, Crouse Hinds Co. of Canada Ltd. and the Dominion Life Assurance Co.

One little-known legacy of Carl and Helen Pollock is Westgate Walk, a one-block cul-de-sac abutting Westmount Golf and Country Club on the border between Kitchener and Waterloo. They built a new house at the end closest to the golf club and moved there from the home on Stirling Avenue North in Kitchener.

On July 3, 1980, two years after his death, Central Ontario Television Ltd. was re-named CAP Communications, to perpetuate his memory. A bust of C.A. by Toronto sculptor Ziggy Puchta stands in the foyer of CAP Communications in Kitchener.

Governor-General Jules Leger installs Carl Pollock as a member of the Order of Canada in 1975.

CHAPTER EIGHT

1981-1989 New Directions

Major investments were made in Electrohome's broadcasting interests in the 1980s, including this news set at CKCO-TV (left).

Specialized high resolution monitors, like the ECM 1301 (above), became another major product line.

The Eighties began with the discovery of major gold deposits in the Hemlo region of northern Ontario, triggering the biggest gold rush in Canadian history. The decade closed with a free trade agreement with the United States which promised new levels of prosperity.

Television made us front row spectators to such memory-searing events as the Challenger space shuttle disaster, the first Canadian in space, Marc Garneau, the fun of the Calgary Winter Olympics and Ben Johnson's disgrace.

The Eighties opened with a bang for Electrohome. Record sales and profits in the first two years created a sense of confidence that the company was heading in the right direction. The $15.8 million in profits from 1980 were followed by $8.6 million in 1981.

But the results were a smokescreen. In the five years from 1977 to 1982, the company's survival rested largely on the success of an unlikely "white knight"—the coin-operated video games business. In a remarkable sequence of events, Electrohome found a market for its monitor-making expertise among manufacturers of such video games as Asteroids and Pacman. Sales of $122 million contributed significantly to the bottom line during this five-year span (*see Asteroids, Pacman & Electrohome, page 137*).

But when the video game bubble burst, Electrohome's management team found themselves once again facing losses. Ahead lurked a decade of turbulence and change, fuelled by a fluctuating world economy and a major recession. The company was driven from its traditional position as a consumer goods manufacturer into areas of advanced technology that were only a dream when Carl Pollock was at the helm.

While difficult, the fundamental changes undertaken during this period were essential to the company's survival.

Over 50 high performance Electrohome color monitors were installed at Cape Canaveral's media centre for launch of space shuttle Columbia carrying the Canadarm for the first time.

Although they were a complete departure from the company's roots, the new directions undertaken by the third generation of the Pollock family were in step with the changing times but were nevertheless a challenging reality faced by Electrohome and many other companies during the 1980s.

At the close of the decade, John Pollock was to describe the Eighties as a period of dramatic and sustained change. It was a restrained description of a series of events which had subjected him to agonizing soul-searching in the face of inescapably tough decisions.

The fateful slide down the slippery slope of change began in the last three months of 1981 as the recession began to take its toll. High interest rates kept consumers from spending, leaving Electrohome with large stocks of unsold furniture, TV sets and air moving appliances. This increased the company's level of debt and despite higher overall revenues caused a bigger-than-expected drop in profits.

The first three months of 1982 told the same story: higher sales but lower profits. A company statement summed up the situation: "Consumer spending has fallen dramatically, resulting in major sales reductions and the curtailment of production levels with associated losses. Even service customers are spending only as required and not for preventive maintenance."

Electrohome's industrial and communications businesses were effectively carrying consumer products. The company's successful foray into the video games business provided some much-needed cash flow to counteract the decline in revenue from consumer products.

It was obvious that the time for drastic action had arrived. Electrohome had no choice but to get out of manufacturing consumer products.

The first step in this process came in February 1982, with the sale of the humidifier and dehumidifier business to W.C. Woods Company in nearby Guelph. KeepRite Inc. of Brantford, Ontario, which had made the company's air conditioners for years, bought the rights to use the Electrohome name, a leader in Canadian air moving appliance retail sales.

A few months later, Electrohome announced its withdrawal from the home entertainment business—the business upon which the company was originally based. The agreement with JVC was cancelled after the Japanese manufacturer decided to build a plant in New Jersey to make its own TV sets and other electronic products.

Marketing rights to the Electrohome name for television and audio products were then sold to Melkit Sales Canada Ltd., a new Canadian company established by Mitsubishi Electric Corp., a major Japanese consumer electronics manufacturer.

The only vestige left of the company's once-proud TV business was a contract to assemble about 70,000 color TV sets a year for Melkit at the Wellington Street plant. They bore both the Electrohome and Mitsubishi names with the Electrohome brand being the better seller,

a source of some ironic satisfaction to John Pollock.

The only consumer business left was furniture and it was struggling. So, too, was Service Electrohome. The division was renamed AABEX Electronic Services to project an image of specialized service for computer customers and to service other name brands of household products. While sales increased, high costs were incurred for the re-identification program, upgrading of electronic data processing system and staff retraining.

Despite the gloomy economic situation, the company mounted a major celebration of its 75th anniversary in the spring of 1982. Kitchener's Centre in the Square was the focal point for a program organized by a committee headed by Don Sykes. It included a series of pops concerts by the Kitchener-Waterloo Symphony, attended by over 4,000 employees, shareholders, suppliers, customers and guests.

A company-sponsored exhibition of antique furniture and artifacts, entitled *A Provincial Elegance*, was mounted at the Kitchener-Waterloo Art Gallery and seen by 7,000 visitors.

Our Seventy Fifth Year
75
ELECTROHOME

An exhibition of antique furniture and symphony concerts were part of the 75th anniversary celebrations.

At the company's annual meeting, held in the Centre's main auditorium, John Pollock gave special recognition to Alex Welker, by then a frail 99-year-old. A month later, Welker died.

The recessionary economy continued throughout 1982. Layoffs reduced the workforce from 2,740 to 2,350. Pay increases—which in 1981 had been as high as 14 per cent—were limited to six per cent and the work week extended from 37 1/2 to 40 hours. Each operation adopted its own plan to reduce costs from "stop-start" manufacturing schedules to work sharing.

Before the end of the year, the company had sold off the environmental systems division to Zenon Environmental Inc. of Burlington, Ont., which specialized in this field. It was another sign of the move toward becoming a more focused company.

Monochrome and color display monitors were made for use in public information displays, process control, business graphics, education and personal computers.

The 1982 financial statement summed up the effects of the recession. Sales dropped 15 per cent to $196.3 million. But much worse, profits were non-existent. From a profit of $8.6 million in 1981, the company lost close to $1.1 million. Consumer sales, which 10 years earlier had accounted for 80 per cent of revenue, were down to 18 per cent. Industrial sales were now the biggest revenue generator at 71 per cent, with communications at 11 per cent.

At the annual meeting, John Pollock called the major restructuring that had taken place "a continuation of a move from a consumer-oriented corporation to an enterprise with a more balanced base. The company can now focus on opportunities where we have special capabilities and expertise."

Immediately after the meeting, Stewart Maclellan resigned to join another Canadian-based company. John Pollock, as chairman and chief executive officer, was once more in full control of the company.

Despite the loss, the need to strengthen its position in the remaining businesses resulted in the investment of $11.4 million in research and development of new products and in new production facilities.

A new plant for Planar Circuits in St. Catharines increased Electrohome's printed circuit board manufacturing capacity.

These included a start on the construction of a $2.8 million automated plant in St. Catharines, called Planar Circuits, to make double-sided printed circuit boards. With the single-sided boards made at the Lightning Circuits operation in Niagara-on-the-Lake, the company would have a breadth of product line second to none in Canada.

To capitalize on the video games monitor business coming from the United States, the company established an assembly and distribution plant in Morristown, Tennessee, which opened in April 1982 with 50 employees.

CAP Communications was another area benefitting from new investment. Over $4.5 million had been spent in new facilities and equipment over the previous two years. This helped the station achieve another solid year

a $6 million order from a major U.S. distributor. The relationship, however, lasted only two years. In 1984, Electrohome decided to pursue market opportunities on its own and sold its interest in Gensat to Meridian Technologies Inc.

Another short-lived venture was the Canadian-government Telidon project which had begun with optimistic predictions in the mid-1970s but which ended in disappointment a few years later.

The concept, which in retrospect seemed like a forerunner of the Internet of the Nineties, was to enable consumers, according to a newspaper report, to "delve into a special computerized information system with a flick of their fingers" and view it on a TV-like screen.

A Canadian government spokesman said "viewers can punch special codes into their keypads and watch their screens light up with information contributed to the computer by the *Washington Post, The Washington Star*, the Smithsonian Institute and several government departments."

with a $2 million increase in advertising sales.

In addition to producing a popular children's show, *Romper Room*, and the annual Oktoberfest Parade for the CTV Network, the station had also been responsible for televising Skate Canada '82 and the CIAU basketball championships.

CAP had also entered into a joint venture called Video-Q Systems, which produced and sold video-only commercials for display on TV monitors in 50 Toronto-area supermarkets. After two years, CAP bought out its partner to own the business outright.

The emerging satellite dish television market in the United States and other countries offered an opportunity to employ the company's high-tech capabilities. A joint venture corporation, Gensat Communications Corp., was created with Microdesign Limited of Toronto, to make satellite receivers for home use.

The new company got off to a promising start with

Electrohome received a contract to make the decoder terminals and screens required for the system which was intended eventually to be a two-way interactive system. Sales were announced in the United States to the Corporation for Public Broadcasting, the National Telecommunications and Information Administration and the Department of Health, Education and Welfare. In Canada, the system was being tested by TV Ontario and Bell Canada announced an experiment with a 1,000-unit trial system in Toronto.

These announcements brought ecstatic predictions of skyrocketing sales for Electrohome. Herbert LaPier, head of the electronics division, envisioned Telidon sales going from $3 million in 1981 to $25 million in 1982 and as high as $100 million down the road. The predictions did not materialize and the Telidon project was abandoned by the Canadian government.

The experience, however, led to Electrohome becoming a leader in the manufacture of videotex hardware. In 1984, the company applied its Telidon expertise in developing the EGT-100 decoder, which transformed a television set into a videotex terminal and personal computer. A major customer was a Chicago-area electronic publishing company which used the technology to distribute a broadly-based information service.

The venture was an indication of the volatility of market opportunities governed by rapidly-evolving technology and showed that in such dynamic times there was always something learned that could be applied to another product or another market.

It was also the time when "market niche" entered the language to describe market opportunities—usually resulting from new technology—for products designed specifically to a customer's requirements and manufactured in relatively small quantities.

Herb LaPier started with the company in 1955 as an electronics technician and held several management positions, including vice-president and general manager (1980), vice-president electronics (1982), vice-president operations (1984), and vice-president, Electrohome Ltd., and group vice-president motors (1989). He retired in 1989.

In one sense, this was not a new concept for Electrohome, which for years had made private brand consumer products labelled for specific customers, such as the Viking label for Eatons. Short runs of specially designed electronic displays were often produced during this period.

The major difference in the niche markets of the Eighties lay in the quantities involved. Having been undersold by offshore competitors in the large volume consumer electronics field, the company was beginning to adapt its expertise and production facilities to markets in which large volume manufacturers had no interest.

In the changing Canadian economic climate, it was a strategy being adopted not only by Electrohome but numerous other Canadian companies.

Sub-fractional electric motors being installed in fan heaters at Cambridge plant. This business was also sold in 1989.

At the same time, the company continued to struggle with the effects of the recession. Losses in 1983 shot up to $3.3 million on sales which had declined by $53 million, due largely to the loss of the video game display business.

By the end of 1983, however, the recession appeared to be ending. Consumers cautiously resumed spending, resulting in increased sales of Deilcraft furniture in 1984. Contract sales of television cabinets and hotel furniture

Four design awards were presented to Deilcraft furniture at the 1984 Toronto Furniture Show. Holding awards are (left to right) John Pollock, Gerry McDonnell, general manager furniture; D. Desaulnier, Deilcraft product manager; and Herb LaPier, vice-president, operations.

brought laid-off employees back to work. A return to classic styles resulted in four Trillium Awards for occasional tables and dining suites at the Canadian Furniture Show. A new Deilcraft curio cabinet was selected as the best overall design in the show.

The results for 1984 were encouraging: A small profit, $1.2 million, on sales of $134.8 million. The company's shares rebounded on the Toronto Stock Market from a low of $2.30 up to $6—still a far cry from the 1981 high of $38.

The following year, results were even better as the economic climate improved and consumer spending increased. Sales were $154.4 million and profits $2.6 million. The addition of tax credits increased total profit to $4 million. Share prices reached a high of $9.

Taking stock at this mid-point of the Eighties, John Pollock pointed to the company's sizeable commitments to research and development. Almost $10 million had been invested during the previous two years, most of it on developing new products, including advanced color projection systems. The most notable was the ECP 1000,

a single lens color data and graphics video projector. The first of its kind in the world, it was introduced to hundreds of Fortune 500 company representatives during a 10-week "road show" in 16 major markets across the United States.

The show was organized by David Lowater in conjunction with the Canadian government, which made available its consulates and the Canadian Embassy in Washington.

Projection products were being sold in 26 countries and underlined the growing importance of export sales. Most of the $19.6 million in increased sales in 1985 had come from outside Canada.

The electronics division was a significant contributor to export sales. The division had been reorganized into six separate sectors, each run as an independent business, responsible for its own planning, engineering, manufacturing, sales and profitability. In addition to projection products, growth was recorded by display systems, communications products, printed circuit boards, contract manufacturing and metal stampings.

This single lens projector, the ECP series, was a world first when introduced in 1987.

The metal stampings business had received a boost with a contract to make postal boxes for the Canadian government. This proved to be a market with significant potential with tens of thousand of the boxes being manufactured over several years.

The move away from products and services aimed at the consumer was emphasized once more when a contract to assemble TV sets for Mitsubishi was not renewed because the Japanese company built its own manufacturing plant in Waterloo. About 40 employees lost their jobs.

This was the last TV set made by Electrohome after the contract with Mitsubishi was not renewed in 1986.

All that was left of a once-major consumer manufacturing operation was the Deilcraft furniture division, with AABEX Services retaining a toehold by servicing consumer products.

For Deilcraft, a drop in retail sales resulting from the recession had prompted a search for new markets. These included exports to U.S. dealers, the addition of juvenile furniture, and contract furniture sales to major hotels. As a result of this initiative, elegant Deilcraft designs graced the guest rooms of many well-known

Deilcraft furniture found new markets, including major hotel chains.

hotels, including the Vancouver Meridian, Dallas Four Seasons and Chicago Ambassador.

The motor division was in a state of transition. All DC motor manufacturing was concentrated at the Tennessee plant. After the loss of the video game monitor business, it was decided to enlarge the plant and convert it for electric motor manufacturing. This left the Cambridge plant to supply primarily the mostly-Canadian market for AC motors, which included new motors for frost-free refrigerators and microwave ovens.

The company's relations with its employees had suffered as a result of the uncertainties that had characterized the past few years. Job-sharing programs and layoffs fostered fear and frustration and a series of strikes and walkouts made newspaper headlines. An attempt by the Canadian Auto Workers Union to replace the

International Brotherhood of Electrical Workers was unsuccessful but disruptive. And workers at the Cambridge motor plant publicly expressed their nervousness about the future of their jobs in the wake of the company's move to Tennessee, particularly after the company said labor costs would be cut by 30 per cent as a result of the move.

To improve communications with the staff, John

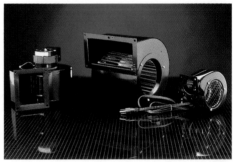

Pollock initiated a series of informal lunch meetings, inviting employees selected at random from all departments to share their views with him.

AC motors drove these blowers used in numerous air moving applications.

While investing time in keeping the lines of communication open, John Pollock had far more serious problems facing him in the last half of the Eighties. The profitable results of 1984 and 1985 proved to be a lull before the storm which had been brewing for some years.

Losses of $7.2 million in the next two years forced the company into making some serious decisions that ultimately pointed the way to the company's future directions. By the end of the Eighties, the company was completely out of the consumer products business.

Gone were Deilcraft furniture, AABEX Service and the motors division—all sold as going concerns to other companies in the same fields which presumably would

Informal lunch meetings with employees were initiated by John Pollock to improve communications.

be able allocate the resources required to survive in the changing business climate of the late Eighties and the coming Nineties.

For John Pollock, the decisions were painful. He was faced with abandoning businesses created by his grandfather and father and built by several generations of craftsmen and women.

But there really was no choice in the face of unrelenting evidence that the company's resources should be invested in broadcasting and commercial video electronic products, instead of the much riskier historic business fields. That evidence included the fact that most of the companies which had been Electrohome's direct competition, including Admiral, Philco, General Electric, Sylvania, Fleetwood, Westinghouse and Clairtone, had either left the consumer products field, been closed, sold or gone bankrupt.

CKCO-TV news crew was selected to bring CTV network viewers the medal presentations at 1988 Calgary Winter Olympics.

As losses again began to mount in 1987, further tough decisions were made. John Pollock later reflected that more changes took place in 1987 than in any 12-month period in the company's 80-year history.

AABEX Electronic Service was sold, a victim in part of declining business because of the increased reliability of consumer products, particularly color TV sets. A year later, CAP Communications sold Video-Q Marketplace Television.

The biggest shock to many was the sale of the Deilcraft furniture division at the end of 1987 to Brian and Tom Callahan of Toronto, representing a group of investors.

The Callahans also owned Barrymore Furniture Ltd., a manufacturer of high quality upholstered furniture established in Toronto around the turn of the century. Their purchase included the Kitchener and Milverton plants with 440 employees, as well as warehouses and showrooms in Kitchener, Toronto and North Carolina.

In 1987, there had been no intention of disposing of the motor division. In fact, expansion was in the air with the acquisition of the Brinkley Motor Products Company of Brinkley, Arkansas, a company specializing in AC motor production.

The purchase, said the company, "reaffirmed Electrohome's commitment to the sub-fractional motor business." At this point, the motor division consisted of three plants: The new Brinkley plant, 90,000 square foot, employing 145 people; the 50,000 square foot plant in Morristown, Tennessee, with 150 people; and the 125,000 square foot Cambridge plant employing 300 people.

Despite aggressive and reasonably successful moves to increase business, the motor division continued to be economically marginal.

In the end, it was decided that adequate returns were not possible in the face of competition from other North American motor manufacturers five or six times larger.

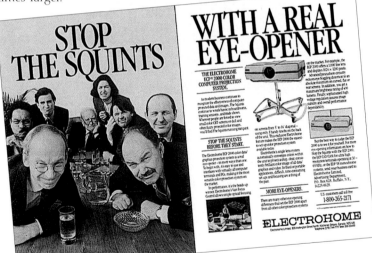

As other business segments were sold, sales and marketing efforts for projection systems were stepped up.

In December 1989, the three-factory business was sold to Fasco Industries Inc., an American subsidiary of Hawker Siddeley of England, for $11.5 million.

With the sale of these businesses, the company was

free to concentrate on the two business segments on which its future was to be based: Broadcasting and commercial video electronic products.

Sunwapta Broadcasting of Edmonton was acquired in 1988. The long-established company consisted of a TV station and two radio stations.

The company's investment in broadcasting—historically its most consistently profitable area of business—was doubled in April 1988 when Electrohome bought Sunwapta Broadcasting of Edmonton for $53 million.

Sunwapta, which owned CFRN-TV and two associated radio stations, CFRN-AM and CKXM-FM, was bought from Dr. G.R.A. (Dick) Rice, who started the company in 1934 with a small AM radio station and built it into one of the largest broadcasting operations in western Canada.

The purchase gave Electrohome a second broadcasting operation, almost identical to CKCO-TV in Kitchener-Waterloo. Both were part of the CTV Network, both incorporated AM and FM radio stations and each had approximately 200 employees.

The purchase culminated 17 years of on-and-off discussions and negotiations between Dick Rice, Bill McGregor and John Pollock.

Dr. Rice, then in his late 80s, stayed on as honorary chairman of a new board of directors which included four Alberta residents: Bruce Campbell, an Edmonton city council member; Lois Field, a community health nurse; Jan Miller, co-artistic director of Small Change Theatre and national co-ordinator of the National Screen Institute of Canada; and Dr. John L. Schlosser, chairman of the University of Alberta board of governors. John Pollock became chairman and Bill McGregor, vice-chairman.

The purchase was followed by an investment of $12 million on a new building and new equipment for the Edmonton operation and state-of-the-art digital video recorders at both TV stations.

Major investments in broadcasting operations included a new control room at CKCO-TV.

The Edmonton acquisition made Electrohome's broadcasting arm the third-largest CTV network affiliate behind Baton Broadcasting (CFTO-TV) in Toronto and WIC Western Communications Ltd. of Vancouver. It also made broadcasting the company's largest area of investment at 69 per cent. Since broadcasting had historically been more profitable than manufacturing, the expansion was expected to contribute substantially to Electrohome's profitability.

Hand-held control was one of advanced features of large-screen color video projection systems pioneered by Electrohome engineers.

The Commercial Electronics division, in the meantime, had been reorganized into four business sectors: Projection Systems, Display Systems, a digital commercial video operation called Jazz Systems, and Component Products, which included the two printed circuit board operations.

Unlike the totally domestic-oriented broadcasting operation, electronics was competing in a global marketplace against many well-recognized world class brand names. This required a constant search for new products and services to meet ever-changing customer requirements.

One example was the way the company responded to a customer's need for a more user-friendly operation of a large screen color video projection systems for data and graphics. Electrohome engineers, who were pioneers in this field, made the system controllable through a new computerized hand-held control. The advances both satisfied customer expectations and increased sales.

Display Systems concentrated on a few markets with better-than-average potential and successfully sold monochrome and color monitors for use in financial trading houses, public information displays, medical imaging and graphics.

In 1989, the company made a strategic alliance with a British firm, Microvitec Ltd., which had considerable expertise in manufacturing color displays. By combining manufacturing and marketing skills, the alliance resulted in Electrohome concentrating on sales to the Americas and Microvitec being responsible for sales in Britain and Europe.

The new venture, Jazz Systems, was developed to sell a unique digital video effects unit to video production houses including corporate, videographic and cable groups, and broadcast edit suites.

The Component Products sector included the circuit board operations in St. Catharines and Niagara-on-the-Lake, and the Kitchener metals operation based in the original Victoria Street plant. Despite investing in computer-controlled equipment to improve efficiency and increase the plant's capabilities, the metals operation was struggling to achieve satisfactory profit levels with its Canada Post contracts.

Unique digital video-effects were created by Electrohome's Jazz Systems.

The re-positioning of the company in the Eighties was not achieved without pain. On the human relations level, the workforce went from 2,500 in 1980 to 1,600 in 1989. Sales during the decade had ricocheted from a high of $232.2 million to a low of $142 million.

Share prices reflected the ebb and flow of the company's profitability as it struggled with the

ECP 3000 projectors used in a driver simulator at Hughes Aircraft in California.

had risen by a healthy 10 per cent to $178.5 million, almost half of which were to customers outside Canada.

In his 1989 report to shareholders, John Pollock acknowledged the company's "unsatisfactory financial

performance" of the past decade.

On an optimistic note, he said the company's move from seven businesses to two "is in step with today's evolving economic patterns. Our long-term stability has been strengthened and our future is now focused on areas where we have acknowledged expertise.

"With the opportunity to focus on two relatively fast-moving businesses, I am confident that significant progress is now possible. We enter the new decade in a much healthier condition and with a more positive outlook that was the case 10 years ago. We look to the future with much anticipation."

effects of a recession and the realities of the new world economy.

By the end of 1989, however, the company was showing a profit again after three years of losses. Sales

Asteroids, Pacman & Electrohome

Among its many ventures, Electrohome's flirtation with the video game business was probably the most dynamic.

In a span of less than four years, the company experienced sales that rocketed from zero to an annual peak of $74 million and then plummeted back to zero. During this in-and-out experience, Electrohome chartered Boeing 747 cargo jets to keep up with demand.

Doug Wismer, manager of equipment engineering, spent three years cultivating contacts in the rapidly-

Doug Wismer: Uncovered video game market for Electrohome monitors.

unfolding video games business in the late 1970s. He and his wife toured the United States visiting 24 games manufacturers to identify the leaders. "There were seven of them—and we supplied most of them with monitors made to their specifications." They included Midway Manufacturing in Chicago, Gremlin in San Diego, which made Sega games, and Atari.

"There were many people at Electrohome who didn't think the video game business would amount to anything. But John Pollock did and he made sure that money was found—at a time when cash was tight—to keep on funding this business."

The big breakthrough came with an order for a special monochrome monitor for a new coin-operated game being introduced by Atari. It was called Asteroids and in a very short time, it became the most popular video game in the world.

This Asteroids game is now in Electrohome museum in Kitchener.

"The demand was so high that Atari couldn't wait the three days it took a truck to get from Kitchener to California," according to Wismer. "For a few weeks, we shipped the monitors by chartered Boeing 747 cargo jet. We also sent monitors to Atari's European manufacturing facility in Tipperary, Ireland. The only thing that could bump our products off the plane was the Royal Mail."

The success of Asteroids soon moved the industry to using color monitors.

"Atari's engineering manager asked if we could make him a color monitor for a new game called Pacman," recalled Wismer. "We showed it at the next Chicago electronics show and it was a hit. I came home with $25 million in orders."

Electrohome made monitors for seven major games manufacturers. The bonanza was not without its problems, of course. An order for 5,000 monitors made for Gremlin Manufacturing and supplied to Sega, a subsidiary of the Gulf and Western conglomerate, almost became a disaster for Electrohome.

"The new technology we built into the monitor was not fully understood by the end-user and the monitors began to fail. We sent technicians to every location in the United States to fix the problem. We told everyone in the industry what we'd done and what we had learned from the experience. We were very open.

"As a result, we earned a reputation for being the best, even though the problem cost the company about $700,000."

The video games bubble began to burst by mid-1982 as short product runs of specialized monitors were replaced by standardized products supplied by offshore TV set manufacturers eager to cash in on the videogame market.

Faced with dwindling demand, Electrohome was all but out of this business by 1984.

For the five years that it lasted, the video game business provided Electrohome with a healthy injection of profits at a time when it was needed.

"An Old-fashioned Family Deal"

That was how one magazine article described the 1987 purchase by Electrohome of Sunwapta Broadcasting Company Ltd. in Edmonton. It went on to describe how the sale was 15 years in the making, mainly because Sunwapta's owner, Dr. G.R.A. Rice, wanted to sell "his" company to an owner with a similar philosophy to his own.

When Dick Rice met Carl Pollock in the early 1970s, he discovered a kindred spirit with an old fashioned grassroots approach to community broadcasting. The two agreed to give each other the first right of refusal if either decided to sell their broadcasting companies.

Dick Rice, who started his radio career at age 15, began broadcasting in Edmonton in 1922.

Dick Rice and John Pollock

Even though Carl Pollock had died in the meantime, when Dick Rice decided it was time to retire, he turned to Electrohome.

In a statement to his employees announcing the sale, Dick Rice said: "My sincere belief is that CAP Communications is parallel in its philosophy to that of Sunwapta and carries forward the 'human factor' which has been established in our Sunwapta relationship."

Newspaper reports of the sale speculated that Dr. Rice could have sold the company for more than the $53 million paid by Electrohome but "his disdain for mega-sized media conglomerates" influenced his decision.

That would have been typical of a man who was a broadcasting pioneer in western Canada. Born in England, he started his radio career with the Marconi Company at the age of 15. During the First World War, he served with the Marconi British Admiralty Service.

He visited Canada in 1919 and liked the country well enough to return the following year. At the time, the only broadcasting stations in Canada were operated by the Canadian Marconi Company in Montreal and Toronto.

In 1922, he opened CJCA for the Edmonton Journal which he operated for 12 years.

In 1934, he bought another Edmonton station, CTPF in partnership with Hans Neilsen, an Edmonton grocer who saw the benefits of running his advertisements alongside the popular Edgar Bergen and Charlie McCarthy

shows. They renamed the station CFRN, incorporating their last initials. The same initials were used when the company opened Edmonton's first TV station in 1954. The operating company's name, Sunwapta, is a Stoney Indian word meaning rippling or radiating waves.

Sunwapta and Dick Rice won dozens of awards in radio and TV categories. The University of Alberta awarded Dick Rice an honorary doctor of laws degree in 1965 and in 1976, he was honored as the individual making the most significant contribution to Canadian broadcasting. He was president of the Alberta

Pictured at a CFRN Christmas party (left to right): Dick Rice, his first wife, Susan who later died of cancer, and Hans Neilsen, Rice's original partner.

New headquarters of CFRN-TV in Edmonton, built after joining Electrohome.

branch of the Canadian Cancer Society from 1951-54 and was honored in 1951 by the Edmonton branch of the Associated Canadian Travellers for CFRN's support of crippled children.

Looking back over his early days in radio, Dick Rice told of dealing with temperamental microphones. "Microphones were our major headache. When they failed, we never had a replacement handy. We simply made another one."

Dick Rice served as honorary chairman of the Sunwapta board of directors for one year after the Electrohome purchase. He died on February 26, 1992.

John A. Pollock:
Biting The Bullet Of Change

As a young man, John Pollock liked to sit with his father, Carl, and talk about the business.

"We were good friends. We both loved talking about the company."

Today, as chairman and chief executive officer of Electrohome, John Pollock occasionally ponders what his father would say about "the new Electrohome," focussed as it is entirely on two market niches that were in their infancy when C.A. Pollock was at the company's helm.

John Albon Pollock

It was John who had to face the fact that Electrohome could not survive by clinging to the businesses of the past.

"I believe he would have approved of the decisions we made to survive and prosper in a rapidly-changing world. He spent his business career adapting to change and making the most of new opportunities."

John Pollock, born in 1936, grew up in a household that he describes as "comfortable—but conservative." He and his sister, Barbara, (married to a Toronto lawyer who is now a judge), were always conscious of the busy lives led by their father and grandfather, A.B. Pollock.

"We would be taken to grandfather's (Benton Street) house every Saturday and greeted by a Mennonite maid, Mattie. In the music room, we would listen to Grandmother sing and play the piano. She also entertained us at the cottage in Muskoka, where we spent the summers."

C.A. would drive up each weekend and honk his car horn from the mainland when he arrived. A boat would be dispatched to bring him to the island cottage.

John and sister, Barbara, with their parents, Carl and Helen Pollock, at Muskoka family cottage.

John remembers his father driving them to the cottage in a small LaSalle in the 1940s. "It was a dirt road beyond Guelph." After the war, there was a black and yellow Morris Minor which John was allowed to drive when he reached the age of 15.

"Then I drove a Hillman convertible around North America on a six-week holiday before I went to University."

"I believe Dad always assumed I would go into the business. As a youngster, I'd go to the Duke Street plant with him on the weekends and have fun riding the conveyor systems while he worked."

When fire struck the plant in 1952, John helped with the cleanup. While at K-W Collegiate and later at Ridley College in St. Catharines, he spent his summers working at one of the plants.

"One of my first jobs was carrying core veneers. I learned the hard way that unless I wore gloves, my hands would be filled with slivers. I was paid 45 cents an hour and earned a premium on piecework...I was one of the boys."

Later he worked in the motor division on Victoria Street, building and repairing electric motors. This was followed by time study work and building sample products in the engineering department.

While studying engineering at the University of Toronto, he spent a summer laying out pole lines and surveying for Bell Canada's plant engineering department.

He also worked in England for two engineering companies which supplied Electrohome with specialized products.

After graduating with a Bachelor of Science degree in engineering in 1959, John worked at Eaton's downtown Toronto store for a year, learning the retail business from a valued customer. "I sold everything from boats to small appliances, TVs and stereos." Within five months, he was one of Eaton's top four salesmen in the home entertainment department.

Then he spent five months travelling around the

John Pollock was 24 when he made a five-month trip around the world. Here he is in the Valley of the Kings along the Nile River, Egypt.

world on his own. He paid for it by selling an old Jaguar car he bought from his father following university. "I sold it for $2,000 and used the money to pay for an around-the-world airline ticket." He had a $10 a day budget for meals, accommodation, phone calls, gifts—everything. "In Egypt, I paid 35 cents a night to sleep on King Farouk's cook boat on the Nile. It was a memorable trip."

On his return he went to Harvard and obtained an MBA degree. In his second year, during a skiing holiday in Stowe, Vermont, he met his future wife, Joyce, who lived in Concord, Mass. After graduating in English from the University of Wisconsin, she went on to pursue studies in music at the New England Conservatory. They were married eight months later and returned to Canada in 1962. They have four adult children, Kimberlee S., Kristen A., Nichola C. and Graham J.A.

director of Canadian General Tower Ltd. of Cambridge; Budd Canada Inc. of Kitchener and S.C. Johnson and Son, Brantford. Other interests have included Manufacturers Hanover Bank of Canada, Toronto; Canstar Sports Inc. and Waterloo Scientific Inc.

He has undertaken numerous volunteer positions including serving on the board of governors of the University of Waterloo and as board chairman of an independent school. He is a past member of the Science Council of Canada and headed an advisory council for the School of International Business based at the University of Western Ontario. He is a past president of the Kitchener-Waterloo Art Gallery and has served on the boards of the Canadian Clay and Glass Gallery and Freeport Hospital. He was appointed by the Ontario Government to serve on the board of the Trillium Foundation, a provincially-funded grants organization, which he served for six years.

He has also participated at many levels in numerous industry organizations, including his current involvement as a member of the CTV board of directors.

Together, he and his wife share a love for gardening with a particular interest in trees. They still spend time with their children and grandchildren at the summer cottage that was brought into the family by John's grandfather five generations ago. John enjoys sailing and skiing and, despite a heavy international business travel schedule, he and Joyce enjoy travelling for pleasure.

John joined the company as assistant to Leo Fitzpatrick, then consumer products sales manager. This was followed by positions in marketing, product development and sales management, primarily in consumer products and then a series of positions in general management.

John Pollock took over as president in 1971 when C.A. decided to step back from the day-to-day running of the company. He became chairman in 1980 and chairman and chief executive officer in 1981. He is also a

1990-1997 The New Electrohome

The optimism expressed by John Pollock as he looked forward to the 1990s was not to be rewarded immediately.

The company's path to a profitable recovery ran into the roadblock of another worldwide recession which quickly made the free-spending days of the late Eighties a profligate memory.

The world turned to cost-cutting, downsizing and "doing more with less." Canadians knew things were bad when tens of thousands of employees of blue chip companies and those with "safe" government jobs found themselves facing layoffs or being offered early retirement packages

That was the bad news. The worse news, according to many economic commentators, was that in the evolving economic order, most of the jobs would never return. The daily litany of bad news generated nervousness and uncertainty.

"The enthusiasm and promise that normally surrounds the start of a new decade was dampened by the recession that is part of the current economic environment throughout North America," John Pollock told shareholders.

The slumping economy hit Electrohome in a number of ways.

For the broadcasting group, the first signs appeared in the fall of 1990 when advertising sales did not rebound after the usual summer doldrums. Consumers, not sure how long they would have a job, stopped making purchases–houses, furniture, almost anything. Retailers cut back on advertising or looked at less costly ways of attracting customers.

Don Willcox, who had succeeded Bill McGregor as vice-president and general manager of CKCO-TV in 1989, reported declining sales in the Ontario marketplace. His CFRN-TV counterpart, Bruce Cowie, told a similar story. According to the annual report, "1990 was not a vintage year for broadcasters."

This downturn in broadcasting could not have come at a worse time. The company had just invested $65 million in the purchase of Sunwapta in Edmonton and the subsequent expansion and upgrading of facilities and equipment.

For the company's electronics business, the recession had a mixed effect with some products experiencing strong demand and others reflecting customer reluctance to invest in new technology. For example, monitor sales softened because of a decline in financial trading markets.

The financial picture at the end of 1990 showed an overall sales increase of $3 million but a major drop in profits.

The financial statement was severely affected by the bankruptcy of the company which had bought the Deilcraft furniture division. Electrohome was left holding a $3.6 million promissory note and was forced to write it off, converting the year's operating profit of $249,000 into a $3.3 million loss.

The continuing recession forced the company into

Don Willcox, vice-president and general manager of CKCO, 1989.

the same kind of intense self-scrutiny being undertaken by most organizations in their search for a survival strategy. The result was another round of restructuring which started early in 1992.

First to go was the metal products division, one of the early spinoffs of the original phonograph business. MHS Metal Products Inc., a new company, bought the business and equipment and agreed to hire the existing workforce at current wage levels and benefits. Ownership of the land and buildings was retained by Electrohome.

Next was the digital video business, Jazz Systems, a relatively new addition to the Electrohome family, which had lost money because of a severely depressed market for broadcast equipment. It was sold to a company which specialized in this field.

The biggest move was the sale of the company's four radio stations in Edmonton and Kitchener. Both AM and FM stations in each market had undertaken "repositioning" transformations in an attempt to increase their share of listenership and after aggressive promotion were showing signs of success.

Their improved profitability made them an attractive purchase but the Kitchener sale ran into problems with the original buyer. Another buyer was found and by the end of 1993 Electrohome was no longer in the radio broadcasting business. Another long-time interest of the Pollock family had fallen victim to a changing economy.

Don Willcox retired in 1995 after 35 years with CKKW Radio and CKCO-TV. Shortly before retiring, he was presented with the Howard Caine Memorial Award in recognition of his community service work. He was succeeded by Dennis Watson, who joined the company from CHEX-TV in Peterborough, Ontario in a similar position to that filled by Fred Filthaut at CFRN in 1993.

It was also decided to get out of the printed circuit board business. Planar Circuits, which made double-sided boards in St. Catharines, was sold in 1992. Lightning Circuits, the single-sided circuit board manufacturing plant in Niagara-on-the-Lake, went in mid-1993.

Overall, the sale of these businesses gave the company an influx of cash totalling $14.3 million. Most of this went to reducing debt, which had been concerning the company's bankers. At the end of 1990, the company had been technically in default on loans with its two bankers. After reviewing the company's proposals to cut costs and raise money by selling business segments, the banks agreed to waive the defaults and restructure the loans, at significant additional cost to the company.

To add management expertise to the organization, the directors appointed Zoltan D. Simo, a businessman who had been a board member since 1988, as president and chief executive officer. He cut costs by eliminating layers of middle management, a tough issue that had been avoided, according to one senior manager.

His mission accomplished, Simo resigned as president in March 1993 and John Pollock again became chief executive officer as well as chairman. Bill McGregor was appointed senior vice-president and elected to the board of directors. Daniel Wright was made vice-president and chief financial officer.

The two operating businesses were made into autonomous groups, each with its own president and chief operating officer. Two long-serving senior executives were appointed to run them: Bruce Cowie, broadcasting, and David Lowater, electronics.

With a new management team in place, a leaner organization and a general economic improvement, the company reported net earnings of $8.6 million for 1993. Late in 1993, the company changed banks, appointing the Canadian Imperial Bank of Commerce for its broadcasting business and the Bank of Montreal for electronics.

The new Electrohome was ready to face a future that showed a lot more promise than was evident at the beginning of the decade.

Both business groups made significant progress as the economy eased out of the recession.

The broadcast group showed steady sales levels and earnings, despite dire predictions of the impact on viewership of competition from a growing number of sources.

Both TV stations used new state-of-the-art news-gathering and presentation equipment to upgrade local programming and increase viewership. Programs produced by each station were shown on the CTV network and sold to specialty channels in the United States, Middle East and Japan.

Late in 1995, Electrohome signed a strategic alliance agreement with Baton Broadcasting Inc., a major shareholder in the CTV network controlled by the Eaton family of department store fame. The agreement envisaged the creation of two jointly-owned broadcasting

(Top)
Bill McGregor,
Daniel Wright,
Bruce Cowie,
and Dave Lowater.

State-of-the-art television control room at Sunwapta.

units which would enable both companies to compete more effectively in the increasingly fragmented television environment.

This agreement was approved by the CRTC but the two companies subsequently negotiated a more comprehensive amalgamation of their TV interests and re-applied for CRTC approval. A decision was expected by late fiscal 1997.

Under the new agreement, Electrohome was to receive approximately $24 million in cash and 8.3 million shares, or about a 23.5 per cent share of the new Baton Broadcasting company.

John Pollock would become co-vice-chairman of the new Baton board and chairman of the executive committee. Electrohome's Bruce Cowie was made executive vice-president and chief operating officer, reporting to Ivan Fecan, the new Baton president and chief executive officer.

Early in 1997, the CRTC—following a hotly-contested competition between five Canadian TV broadcasting companies—awarded a licence for a new station in Vancouver to the Baton-Electrohome alliance.

Soon afterwards, Baton and CHUM Limited negotiated a deal under which Baton TV stations in London, Windsor, Wingham and Pembroke/Ottawa were exchanged for the Maritime CTV group of stations known as ATV. They included stations in Halifax, Sydney,

Moncton/Charlottetown and St. John/Fredericton, as well as the Atlantic Satellite Network cable programming service.

CHUM also received $10 million in cash for its 14.3 percent equity in the CTV network.

If and when these changes are approved by the CRTC, expected in the summer of 1997, the Baton-Electrohome alliance will have coast-to-coast coverage and a 57 per cent controlling interest in the CTV network.

From Electrohome's viewpoint, the company had traded its broadcasting assets for a major stake in a larger and stronger broadcasting company, better positioned for success in an increasingly-fragmented market. In addition to control of the CTV network, Baton has controlling interest in two newly-licensed specialty channels, The Comedy Network and Talk TV, as well as the largest stake in a third channel, Outdoor Life. CTV also received licences for three new specialty channels including News One, an all-news channel expected to be on the air by September 1997.

Withdrawal from active management of its broadcasting interests enabled Electrohome to focus its energies on the promising Visual Communications Group, made up of two divisions, Projection Systems and Display Systems.

Despite the overall downward pull of the recession through the difficult early years of the Nineties, the group's focus on market niches continued to pay off. The Display Systems division, a leader in medical imaging and instrumentation, process control and financial trading rooms, supplied high performance monitors

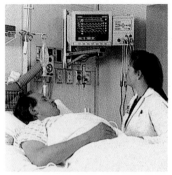

which use liquid crystal displays (LCDs) or cathode ray tubes (CRTs).

A philosophy of "customer intimacy" was adopted to develop close working relationships with customers requiring high levels of product customization, technical support and fast manufacturing turnaround. The company's ability to tailor products to meet customer requirements attracted such high-profile North American customers as General Electric, Allen Bradley and Xycom.

An innovative dual screen LCD color display was developed for Bloomberg Financial Services in New York, and installed in the offices of worldwide subscribers to their financial news service.

Other high-profile Wall Street customers using Electrohome displays include Shearson Lehman, Merrill Lynch, Smith Barney and Morgan Trust.

To strengthen its capabilities in this specialized field, Electrohome bought Display Technologies of Carthage, Missouri, in July 1995. The company, renamed Display Technologies Electrohome (DTE), was a world leader in manufacturing high resolution monochrome displays and was the dominant supplier to the North American document imaging industry.

David Lowater said the addition of DTE—with 220 employees and annual sales of over $25 million—would lead to expansion in the growing market for filmless X-ray imaging and diagnostics.

Strategic alliances with companies with different high technology capabilities created opportunities to develop new products. A partnership with Microvitec

in Bradford, England, enabled Electrohome to attract new business for a wider range of color monitors in a variety of sizes.

These alliances and acquisitions were significant steps along the road to recognition of Electrohome's leadership in supplying visual display systems, according to Bruce Brown, vice-president and general manager of Display Technologies.

Similar positioning was adopted for Projection Systems, headed by Gerry Remers. The pioneering efforts of 1979 had resulted in Electrohome building an enviable reputation as a quality supplier of leading edge projection equipment. Regional sales representatives and a team of field application engineers maintained close contact with system integrators who designed and installed custom applications for training centres, corporate boardrooms, video conferencing rooms and command and control centres.

While some major installations were made in Canada, including Bell Telephone and CN Rail, Electrohome

projection systems had become well known around the world. The customer list includes major corporations and government agencies in 55 countries.

Among a string of noteworthy installations were the Seoul Police Department in South Korea, the Thames Water Board in England, CSX Rail in Jacksonville, Florida, and the Los Angeles Fire Department. Electrohome displays were used in the Los Angeles courtroom during the high-profile trial of former football star O.J. Simpson.

Thanks to a determined effort by the company's Japanese distributors, Nissho Electronics, the company scored a major success by winning a contract to supply projection equipment for the control rooms of Nippon Telephone and Telegraph. It was the first time this Japanese telephone company had bought projectors from outside the country, underlining the significance of this unique accomplishment.

A three-year effort based on building a strong relationship with key AT&T personnel led to a contract to supply 75 projectors for a large video wall used to monitor 140 million telephone calls a day at AT&T's New Jersey nerve centre. The success of this installation led to similar contracts around the world.

In 1994, the division introduced ShowStar, the first in a new generation of high brightness projectors based

Electrohome Retro Projection Systems are used at Thames River London, England, the world's largest water management system.

on LCD technology. The National Bowling Stadium in Reno, Nevada, installed 56 of the projectors to illuminate a continuous wall of screens above the pins on 80 bowling lanes. Subsequent ShowStar installations in the event presentation market include theme parks, sports bars, casinos and many other large audience venues.

A new projection system introduced in 1996 uses digital light processing (DLP), a revolutionary technology from Texas Instruments. Named the Vista Pro series, the system's cinema-like brightness and clarity was designed for the exacting requirements of the rental staging, multimedia and video presentation markets and is expected to solidify Electrohome's position in these expanding fields.

The National Bowling stadium, Reno, Nevada, features a 440 foot wide wall, using 56 projectors.

As Electrohome entered its 90th anniversary year, the results of the restructuring were appearing on the company's financial statements. Despite the ups and downs of a volatile marketplace, revenues were increasing each year and profit levels were improving.

Although the visual communications industry was dominated by electronics giants, Electrohome had carved out a leading position in a rapidly-growing niche product area. David Lowater, president and chief operating officer of the Visual Communications Group, attributed the company's success to "our ability to develop integrated solutions that fit each customer's specific needs."

In addition to increasing exports to the Asia Pacific region, opportunities for both projection systems and display installations are being pursued in Europe, South America and the Middle East, through marketing and distribution operations in Britain, Singapore, California, New York and Missouri.

The transition from being a major consumer products manufacturer with as many as 4,400 employees to a narrowly-focussed producer of visual communications equipment and a major investor in TV broadcasting was difficult and at times painful.

For many who regarded themselves as Electrohome "members," there were only memories of a time that has passed. To hear them reminisce was to conjure up visions of the daily routines, the shared experiences, the friendships, the rivalries and the pride in a job well done.

Today's members of the Electrohome team have their sights firmly fixed on the horizon, where the promises of tomorrow beckon.

During this rapidly-changing period, the entire organization took part in a number of programs aimed at strengthening the capabilities of management and focussing the efforts of the organization at all levels.

Dan Wright's experience with a world-class firm of management consultants gave him the perspective to help forge a new strategic approach for Electrohome. Given a mandate to develop a new set of goals and a strategic plan for the organization, he was able to step back from the ebb and flow of daily routine and explore an expanded vision that would guide the company into the 21st century.

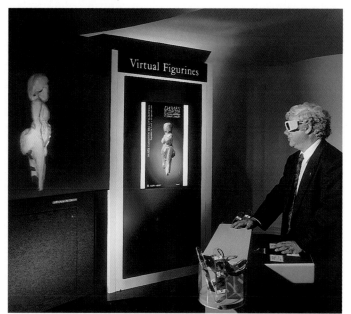

The Canadian Museum of Civilization in Hull, Quebec, projects 3-D images using Electrohome's Marquee® 8000 stereoscopic projector.

The challenge is to chart a path which will allow Electrohome to make the most of its strengths in the rapidly-evolving visual communications marketplace.

Should the company develop new strategic alliances with companies in the same field? Should it take over existing companies or buy a minority interest? Or does the key to success lie in in-house business units specializing in key areas?

The answers to these and many more questions being posed by senior management will be vital to Electrohome's success as the Nineties come to a close.

Equally as vital is the set of shared values which have been forged to guide everyday activities in the workplace. The goal, according to human resources director Brock Hueston, is a program of continuous improvement that will ensure Electrohome's global leadership in visual communications.

Behind the high-tech labels of management in the Nineties are vestiges of the same corporate philosophy which guided A.B. Pollock and his son, Carl.

Their enlightened management approach was a legacy to the third generation which is being continued by John Pollock. No doubt Carl Pollock would smilingly point out that "gain sharing" of the 1990s bears a remarkable similarity to the profit sharing plans he put into place at Electrohome in the 1940s and 1950s.

On the occasion of its 90th anniversary, Electrohome faces a future that is clearly defined, with a strength that comes from having faced and met the challenges of change.

"The transition from our historic roots to a corporation in step with today has been a difficult but successful journey," declared John Pollock.

"The Electrohome team members have done an outstanding job of adapting to rapidly changing business environments. We can look ahead to future growth with confidence knowing that our greatest resources are the inventiveness, dedication, hard work and entrepreneurial spirit of the Electrohome team.

"We have made a positive start on the strategic direction that will take us into the next millennium.

"Change, however, continues to be a fact of life in today's dynamic business environment."

When Arthur B. Pollock founded the company 90 years ago, he set an example which is still being followed today. His ability to recognize the opportunities of a changing marketplace and his determination to be a leader in whatever he undertook are still the values which are driving the company as it marches with confidence into the next century.

Community Support

Bruce Hogle may have retired from CFRN but he's still working hard for the Edmonton TV station's Good Neighbor Fund Society.

This registered charity has raised hundreds of thousands of dollars over the years, all distributed to worthy causes and deserving individuals.

The fund is just one example of the many ways Electrohome people support their local community.

Countless hours are contributed by volunteers working for charities, social service groups and special interest organizations. Employees contribute time as well as money to local United Way and similar broadly based campaigns.

In addition to actively encouraging the efforts of its staff, the company donates a percentage of pre-tax earnings—higher than the national average—to a number of cultural, educational, health and other causes.

(Above left) Electrohome contributed to the establishment of the Woodworking Centre of Ontario at Conestoga College, Kitchener. Shown at a Sod-turning Ceremony September 28, 1988, are (left to right) Doug Kimpe, Chairman of the College Board of Governors; John A. Pollock, George Sinclair, Executive Director, Ontario Furniture Manufacturer's Association; Herb Epp, MPP; and John Tibbits, College President.

CFRN-TV in Edmonton organizes an annual Poor Boy Lunch, a major fund raiser for the station's Good Neighbor Fund.

Electrohome volunteers in Kitchener raise tens of thousands of dollars in the Heart and Stroke Foundation's annual Ride for Heart. The team captured the Golden Wheel Award for three consecutive years for the largest amount of donated money per rider.

1997 Board of Directors

(Seated left to right)
Barbara Steele,
John A. Pollock,
William D. McGregor.
(Standing left to right)
Dr. Douglas T. Wright,
Robert M. Astley,
William E. Hetherington,
George S. Dembroski,
Robert J. Collins-Wright.

Corporate Direction

Our Mission

To advance visual communications through innovative products and services and great television.

Our Vision

Global leadership in visual communications.

Our Values

• **Customers are the centre of our business.**

• **Honesty, Openness and Integrity**

   We're as good as our word.

• **Individual Performance**

   We encourage and help each other to grow.

• **Team Spirit**

   We work together to succeed and share in the results.

• **Continuous Improvement/Total Quality**

   We are committed to delivering forever higher levels of quality, performance and value.

• **Good Management**

   Management has a special responsibility to foster a productive environment where our values can flourish.

Our Beliefs

• We will remain a privately-controlled, Canadian public company.

• We will operate with a blend of mature and growing businesses that address well-defined markets.

• We will provide an adequate return to our shareholders, plus benefits to our employees and the communities in which we are located, through the mutual efforts of the corporation and its most important asset: our people.

Head office and plant employees, Wellington Street North, Kitchener, Ontario, 1996.

A Salute to Electrohome's Quarter Century Club Members

As of June 1997

Active
Cathy Albano
William Alguire
Pat Anthony
Mary Lou Baetz
Mary Anne Baker
Shirley Belkwell
Hannelore Bettinger
Herb Beyerle
Laverne Brohman
Gil Bussman
Marg Cameron
Donald Carthy
Joan Chapman
Joseph Cormier
Julie Dietz
Nick Ditaranto
Donna Farrow
Edward Fronchak
Charlie Fundak
Les Galantai
Gerald Gallagher
Patricia Jiminez
Rosemarie King
Pat Kitchen
Irvin Kretschman
Donald Kurt
Liz Lamont
Richard Lang
Gerry Litwiller
Anne Livingstone
William Lockie
David Lowater
Alfie Lukan
Edward Lukezic
Emma Martin
Ken Meyer
David Morse
Patricia McIlvenna
Donna MacLeod
Joseph Papay
Cecile Pawlak
Kenneth Peplinskie
Tom Phillips
Peter Polfuss
John Pollock
Frank Ramroop
Paul Rehberg
Lydia Reimers

Gord Riggs
Panos Siambanopoulos
Edward Scheinost
Willard Schnarr
Brad Shantz
Pat Shantz
Carl Stather
Miriam Weicker
Barry Weirmier
Doug Wells
Robert Westlake
Carol Westcott
Jadranka Zrnc

Retired Members
Herbert Allgeier
William Appleby
Art Balabazuk
Leopold Baumgart
Michael Bensusan
Fred Bent
Joe Blaskavitch
Ted Bodnar
Don Bonfonte
James Bootle
Paul Bordman
William Bowyer
Yvonne Bricker
Marg Britton
Marilyn Brodrecht
Elmer Brown
Jacob Buhr
William Calma
Marie Cameron
George Canning
Jerome Carey
John Chapeskie
John Chorniawy
Florence Christie
Robert Christner
Doug Clancy
Arthur Coates
Allan Corry
Donald Cousineau
Gord Dalton
Dorothy Daly
Gerard Daly
Angela DeVeau
Stephan Diachyshyn
Bernard Didio
Leonard Dietrich

Conrad Doelle
Eric Donau
Harvey Durst
Helen Dutka
Jacob Dyck
John Dziubinski
Harold Eby
Agnes Ellert
Seb Englert
Eric Enns
Gerhard Fast
Lorne Faulkner
Onolee Feick
Katherine Fischbach
Audrey Fisher
Robert Fleming
Gord Fowler
Shirley Fries
Len Gies
Barb Giilck
James Gillespie
Donald Harrold
Charles Hastings
Roy Hayward
Al Hergott
Eileen Hergott
Ray Hergott
Pola Hickman
Orville Hildebrand
Joseph Horodynski
Ev Ireland
Pat Jutzi
Viola Karius
Joseph Karp
Rita Kennedy
John Kiertscher
Robert Kimmel
Stella Kowtuski
William Krajaefski
Robert Kropf
Rudy Krysko
Elizabeth Kuntzie
Harvey Lammert
Herb LaPier
Al Leasa
Ina Lee
Orville LeVean
Adam Lichacz
Robert Lindsay
Elizabeth Logusch
Robert Lovell

Carl Marschuetz
Ronald Martin
Charles Maurer
Harry Mazurek
Ethel Mewhiney
Waltraud Michi
Fred Molson
Teresa Monaghan
Margaret Moser
Arnold Muma
Gerry McDonnell
Michael MacKenzie
Gerry Nentwig
Alfred Nigul
Frank Nuhn
Edna O'Brien
John Ortinau
Joseph Perlaky
Felicity Petteford
Marg Petzold
Kenneth Pfaff
Robert Pfanner
Walter Pietrzak
Gerhard Poetschke
Sislyn Prince
Jack Pufall
Wes Purvis
Viola Reesor
Tillie Reiner
Isabel Reinhart
Marie Rellinger
Lorne Roberts
Marion Rooke
Alice Roth
Murray Roulston
Les Rowsell
Dorothy Ruth
Lorne Schell
Urban Schell
Elenor Schmidt
Audrey Schneider
Ken Scholl
Stan Schreiter
John Shanahan
Lydia Shantz
Nora Shantz
Myroslow Shewchuck
Ev Shoemaker
Domenico Silvestro
Frank Slota
John Smith

Cam Snider
Leander Soiderer
Jim Sommers
Emil Sonnenburg
Elizabeth Spieker
Katarina Sprach
Hubert Stumpf
Donald Sykes
Cvetko Takov
Ron Thatcher
Keith Thompson
Henry Tikl
George Tomesch
Leonid Trnavskis
Laurine Usher
Harry Verlinden
Alfred Vieregge
Walter Wagester
Lester Wambold
Joseph Wardowski
James Washburn
Eva Wegert
Art Weiler
Harry Wendell
Walter Wood
Robert Woolner
John Wright
Gordon Ziegler
Michael Ziwei

Associate Members
Lloyd Berg
Edith Boensch
Robert Bolden
Martin Bolger
Milton Bordman
Harold Brohman
David Buhlman
Charles Busch
Darwin Chilton
David Christner
Clifford Clive
Carlos Coelho
Charlie Daub
Ronald Dickin
Ray Diefenbaker
Clare Doering
Donald Ducker
Ronald Eckmier
Ken Emmerson
Joseph Eppich

Dennis Erdman
Lyla Faulhafer
Leo Ferneyhough
Dennis Fischer
Robert Flanagan
Leslie Fleiszig
Lyle Foster
Anthony Frattacci
John Fronchak
Ted Fronchak
Arther Getty
Cliff Grant
George Grau
George Grubb
Ervin Hamel
Christian Hehl
Ron Heimpel
William Hess
Shirley Hinsperger
Herb Hoffman
Keith Homuth
Gert (Bob) Jensen
Charles Jonas
Walter Kimpel
John Kleist
Ray Knipping
Siegfried Kopp
Charles Kreutzweiser
Arthur Kropf
Walter Krzewski
Jean Lalonde
Peter Lazin
Marlene Lennox
Wilbert Lichti
Mieczyslaw Ludowicz
Herman Luft
Luiz Macedo
Edna Maier
Nolin Marion
James Martin
Jack Miller
Ernest Missel
Joseph Moser
Lynn McLaughlin
Ronald O'Keeffe
Alois Pfister
Dorthy Pflug
Ina Prior
Glenn Reiner
Mary Lou Reiner
Harold Ruetz

Marlene Knechtel
Steve Savard
Jerome Schumacher
Vynoma Sculthorp
Adam Sienek
Donald Sills
Salvator Silvestro
Robert Simpson
Gertrude Straus
Sandra Straus
Keith Strong
Florian Szozda
Douglas Voisin
Joe Vorstenbosch
Dagmar Wali
Harold Weber
Ronald Witmer
Stan Wrobleski
Allen Zettel
Nick Zienchuk

40 Year Members
Herb Allgeier
William Appleby
Paul Bordman
Marg Britton
William Calma
Dorothy Daly
Gerald Daly
Ray Diefenbaker
Eric Donau
Harvey Durst
Harold Eby
Agnes Ellert
Audrey Fisher
Gord Fowler
Anthony Frattacci
Edward Fronchak
Len Gies
Al Hergott
Ray Hergott
Viola Reesor
Loreen Hurley
John Kiertscher
Art Kropf
Robert Kropf
Rudy Krysko
Al Leasa
Anne Livingstone
Alfie Lukan
Edward Lukezic
Chuck Maurer
Gerry McDonnell
William McGregor
Pat McIlvenna
Fred Molson
Ken Pfaff

Jack Pufall
Wes Purvis
Tillie Reiner
Marie Rellinger
Les Rowsell
Dorothy Ruth
Edward Scheinost
Elenor Schmidt
Ken Scholl
Nora Shantz
Ev Shoemaker
Cam Snider
Hubert Stumpf
Arther Wilder

Deceased Members
Clayton Allgeier
Eileen Austin
Alan Baillie
Lorne Bareham
Clarence Baulk
Ian Bauman
Bruce Baumbach
Bertha Becker
Norman Beisel
Peter Bezruik
William Beith
Orm Boettger
Gordon Braithwaite
Edward Brinkert
Earl Brosowski
John Carnegie
Bert Chapman
Harold Compass
Victor Cook
Eugene Dahmer
Michael David
John Davidson
Edwin Deckert
Elma Detwiller
Graham Dimock
Norman Dippel
Louis Dorscht
Jim Driver
Gladys Eidt
George Eitel
John Egerdeen
Ollie English
Alfred Fercho
Herb Finch
Karl Fischbach
Norman Fischer
Oscar Fischer
Wynfred Fleischauer
Wilfred Frederick
Norman Frey
Josephine Gales

Carl Gies
Eberhard Goetz
Earl Golbeck
William Gromow
Frank Gordon
Emil Gross
Noah Grubb
Robert Hainsworth
Paul Haken
William Hall
Ken Hamilton
Cam Harbridge
Clyde Heimler
Alma Helm
William Hemphill
Vic Hertel
Doug Hilker
Albert Hinschberger
Jerome Hoch
Wilfred Hoefler
Carl Hoffman
Marvin Holtz
John Hummel
Norman Hunt
Carl Jantzi
Walter Jones
Harold Jasper
Don Kehn
Helen Kelly
Harold Kipfer
Ed Klinck
John Koegler
Carl Korell
Clem Kraemer
Stanley Kumornick
Ed Krulicki
Emil Kischnerit
Alfred Lamb
Gord Laronde
Wilhelm Laubenthal
David Leitch
George Leppard
Franny Leyes
Henry Lichodyjewski
Mervin Lichty
Sidney Lichty
Silvio Lieto
John Logozny
August Low
Hermann Lutz
John Maerz
Jack Mahn
Ed Main
Howard Main
Robert Manser
Stanley Miskiewicz
Walter Miskiewicz

Walter Monk
Lorne Moulton
Andy MacIntosh
Jack MacIntosh
Bernadette Murawsky
John Myslywec
Hugh Norris
Peg O'Bright
Albert Orzen
Dominic Paddock
Fred Parker
Jim Pett
Earl Pflug
Arthur Pinke
Arthur Pollock
C.A. Pollock
James Pollock
Harry Pope
Walter Potwarka
John Preidt
Adolph Psutka
Marguerite Ransom
Cleon Reger
Charles Reidel
Ed Reiner
Charles Render
Jack Richardson
Howard Rogers
Harold Rothaupt
Russel Ruppel
Walter Ruppenthal
Marguerite Rush
Albert Sachs
George Schaefer
Clarence Schaub
Edgar Schaub
Howard Schaub
Lorne Schaub
Cyril Schell
Walter Shiel
Robert Schlieman
Karl Schmidt
Leo Seidewand
Garfield Shantz
John Sherk
Ruth Shilling
John Smith
Leo Schisch
Jack Slumkoski
Joe Solomon
Bud Starr
John Stehle
Harry Steinfeldt
Fred Strebel
Bela Stribel
Alfred Stumpf
Peter Tarasuik

Marion Targosz
David Thiessen
John Trautman
J. Gordon Tufts
Merinus Van Ordt
George Vogel
Dorothea Wagner
Eldon Weber
Alex Welker
Lottie Wendt
Hector Wickens
Gord Wilken
Ernest Woelfle
Nick Wojcik
Walter Wytwral
Carl Yager
Albert Zettel
Robert Ziegler

CFRN Television: Active
Robert Anderson
Terry Bartley
Terry Chahley
Dirk Machtans
Ranier Machtans
Brian Marshall
Brenda Martin
Mark Morrison
Jim Napier

Retired Members
Bruce Alloway
Peter Cook
Bruce Hogle
Al Holownia
Bruce Jarron
John Johnson
Dan Kauffman
Peter Leonard
Noreen Lodge
Al McCann
Virginia McCullough
Keith Neale
Bill Radomski
Al Thompson
Diet Velsink
Ted Wadson
Norm Williams
Harold Wojdak

Associate Members
Steve Cox
Jack Little
Graham McLean
Eric Neville
Rod Phillips
Fred Vos

Deceased Members
Dick Rice

CKCO–TV: Active
John Arajs
Elaine Economoff
Laverne Heisz
Bruce Johnston
Paul Nyhout
Earl Pierson
Glenn Toner

Retired Members
Jack Alexander
Dennis Connolly
John Donahue
John Hogben
William Inkol
John Liddle
Donald MacDonald
William McGregor
Joseph McIntyre
Robert McKeown
Gary McLaren
George Moskal
Charles Packham
Reginald Sellner
James Smith
Marvin Stroh
Paul Turchan
Donald Willcox
Harold Zister

Associate Members
Larry Ernewein
Dan Fisher
Henning Grumme
Fred Merritt
Richard Mills
Mary Frances Russell

Deceased Members
Patrick Fitzgerald
Eric Sutherland
Betty Thompson

Electrohome 'Families'

Family connections are a tradition at Electrohome. We were able to find the following families with several generations of Electrohome 'members'.

Allgeier
Clayton Allgeier
Wm Herbert Allgeier
Robert Allgeier
Helen Allqeier
Julie Allgeier
Sandra Allgeier

Brodrecht
Marilyn Brodrecht
Keith Brodrecht
Mike Brodrecht
Ron Brodrecht
Betty Brodrecht

Cormier
Joe Cormier
MaryAnn Cormier
Donna Gaudet
Ulysse Gaudet
Cecile Pawlak
Wally Pawlak
Jeanine Matchett
Bernie Lampke
Jeanette Ruitz
Mike Arsenauld
Ruth Arsenauld
Cloudine Leblanc
MaryAnn Cormier
Vicki Doirion
Richard Leblanc
Maureen Leblanc
Franciss Leblanc
Irene LeBlanc
Theresa LeBlanc

Dalton
Gord Dalton
John Polzin
Agnes Hanner
Bruce Lenanski
Paul Nezny
Eric Donald

Egerdeen
Carol Zinger
Gerry Zinger
Vern Egerdeen
John Egerdeen
Dorothy Strome
Bob Strome
Jane Zeigler
Charles Egerdeen
Brenda Heihn
Patricia Heihn
Heather Heihn
Klara Egerdeen
Shirley Egerdeen

Fishbach
Katherine Fischbach
Karl Fischbach
Peter Fischbach
Carl Fischbach
Lou Fischbach

Flanagan
Bob Flanagan
Frank Flanagan
Ben Flanagan
Dennis Flanagan
Patricia Flanagan
Dawna Flanagan
Theresa Runstedler

Fronchak
Ted Fronchak
Irene Fronchak
Kathy Fronchak
Jeannie Fronchak
Teddy Fronchak
Jerry Litwiller
Joan Litwiller
John Boshart
Ruth Cluthe
William Cluthe
Wayne Smydo
John Fronchak
Terry Fronchak
Cindy Fronchak
Michael Fronchak
Gord Lobsinger
Edmund Lobsinger
Ed Fronchak
Jackie Fronchak
Heather Doucette
Joe Doucette
Jerry Fronchak
Sharon Fronchak
Mary Fronchak

Friedmann
Florence Friedmann
Phyllis Reidl
Tammy Friedmann
Mary Beth
Friedmann
Carolyn Friedmann
Geoff Sheridens
Bradly Caskinette
Dale Cashinelle
Marion Michalik
Doris Wilker

Shirley Ogram
Harry Steinfield
Ria Sheppers

Goetz
Anne Marie Goetz
Frederick Pufall
Agnes Pufall
Clyde Heimler
Jack Pufall
Darryl Baetz

Hergott
Vickie Hergott
Eillen Hergott
Al Hergott
Ray Hergott
Joan Pfaff

Jasper
Harold Jasper
Stanley Jasper
Douglas Jasper
Dorothy Jasper
June Jasper
Hazel Jasper
Shirley Jasper
Craig Hynd
Jamie Hynd

Kropf
George Kropf
Elizabeth
Hoy/Kropf
Art Kropf
Bob Kropf
Albert Kropf
Joan Kropf

Linda Griffin
Terry Kropf
Jim Sommers
Don Kehn
Barbara Hoy
Eddie Hoy
Eldin Willis

Krysko
Rudy Krysko
Michael Krysko
David Krysko
Claye Krysko
Patricia Krysko

Litwiller
Gerald Litwiller
Joan Litwiller
Ronald Litwiller
Janice Litwiller
Chris Yager
Carl Yager
Doug Yager
John Boshart
Irene Fronchak
Ted Fronchak
Ruth Cluthe
William Cluthe

Pollock
Arthur Pollock
Carl Pollock
John Pollock
Barbara Steele
James Pollock
Bob Pollock

Reiner
Edwin Reiner
Shirley Reiner
Bob Dier
Mary Lou Reiner
Glenn Reiner
Pearl Reiner

Rellinger
Marie Rellinger
Joyce Hertel
Gail Dickson
Mary Schwartz
Doreen Eckert
Gary Rellinger
Lynn Rellinger

Schaub
Edgar Schaub
Clarence Schaub
Howard Schaub
Lorne Schaub
Clarence Schaub

Scheinost
August Scheinost
Eric Scheinost
Edward Scheinost
Diane Scheinost
Adolfine Scheinost
Paul Scheinost

Schell
John Schell
Cyril Schell
Urban Schell
Gerrald Schell
Ellinor Schell

Douglas Schell
Don Carthy

Shewchuk
Myro Shewchuk
Audrey Sydor
Mike Shewchuk
Rose Miller
Ann Jarer

Weber
Eldon Weber
Freida Weber
Dzzie Roeric
Ruth Roeric
Wayne Weber
Dianne MacIntoch
David Weber
Stacey Weber
Marilyn Weber
Brent Weber
Don Weber

Weirmier
Barry Weirmier
Ervin Hamel
Linda Hamel
Karl Schmidt
Albert Sacks
Bonnie Evens

Wood
Anne Wood
Claude Wood
Walter Wood
Tom Wood
Jack Maison
Ellen Wood

Bibliography

Company Archives

Advertisements

Alex Welker, taped interview

Board of Directors, minutes

Brochures

C.A. Pollock, notes and public addresses

Catalogues

Financial Statements

John Koegler, research notes

Memorandum Re: Dominion Electrohome Industries
Limited and War Business Re-negotiation

Ontario Credit Union News 21 (1961)

Patents

Press Releases

Radio College News: 1957

Scrap Books

Shareholder Annual Meetings, Shareholder's Reports

Company Publications

Annual Reports, Electrohome Limited

E-World

Sparks and Chips

Sparks and Chips, The Next Generation

Company Histories

Staebler, Edna. *The Electrohome Story: A Canadian Company,
Growing with Canada* (Paris, 1957)

Pollock, Joyce. *History of Electrohome* (1987)
(unpublished manuscript)

General Works

*Berlin, Canada: A Self-portrait of Kitchener, Ontario Before World
War One* (St. Jacobs, 1979)

English, John and Kenneth McLaughlin.
Kitchener: An Illustrated History (Waterloo, 1983, 1996)

Moogk, Edward. *Roll Back the Years* (Ottawa, 1975)

Moyer, Bill. *Kitchener: Yesterday Revisited* (Burlington, 1979)

Nichols, C.M. and John H. Days. *The Twin-City, Berlin and
Waterloo and Their Industries: Commercial, Financial,
Manufacturing.* (Berlin, 1908)

Stanton, Raymond. *Kitchener: A Tradition of Excellence*
(Burlington, 1991)

Uttley, W.V. *A History of Kitchener, Ontario* (Waterloo, 1937)

*Watching TV: Historic Televisions and Memorabilia from the MZTV
Museum,* Liss Jeffrey and Sandra Shaul (editors)
(Toronto, 1995)

Periodicals and Articles

Staebler, H.L. "Random Notes on Music of Nineteenth-
Century Berlin, Ontario." *Waterloo Historical Society* 8 (1949)

Baechler, Glenn. "Waterloo County's Romance with the
Automobile." *Waterloo Historical Society* 59 (1971)

Brenner, Jeff. "The History of the Phonograph."
Waterloo Historical Society 64 (1976)

"52 Years on High School Board." *Waterloo Historical Society* 49
(1962)

Newspapers

Kitchener Daily Record

Kitchener-Waterloo Record
Financial Post
Globe and Mail

Fowler, Gord
Heimler, Clyde
Koegler, John

Interviews by Raymond Stanton, 1996, 1997

Lowater, David
McGregor, W.D.
Pollock, Joyce
Pollock, John
Steele, Barbara,
Sykes, Don
Wismer, Doug
Wright, Dan

Interviews by Nicola McLaughlin, 1996

Harrold, Don
LaPier, Herb
Livingstone, Anne
Lovell, Bob
Lowater, David
Lukan, Alfie
McDonnell, Gerry
McGregor, W.D.
Rowsell, Les
Runge, Walter
Runge, Eileen
Washburn, Jim
Zettel, Al

Interviews by Gary McLaren, 1984

Durst, Harvey
Ellert, Agnes

The history of Electrohome is captured in a mural painted by Christina Peori and portrayed in a prominent location in downtown Kitchener.